Cambridge Practice Tests for First Certificate 2

SELF-STUDY EDITION

Paul Carne
Louise Hashemi and
Barbara Thomas

CAMBRIDGE
UNIVERSITY PRESS

PUBLISHED BY THE PRESS SYNDICATE OF THE UNIVERSITY OF CAMBRIDGE
The Pitt Building, Trumpington Street, Cambridge, United Kingdom

CAMBRIDGE UNIVERSITY PRESS
The Edinburgh Building, Cambridge CB2 2RU, UK   http://www.cup.cam.ac.uk
40 West 20th Street, New York, NY 10011–4211, USA   http://www.cup.org
10 Stamford Road, Oakleigh, Melbourne 3166, Australia
Ruiz de Alarcón 13, 28014 Madrid, Spain

First published 1996
Sixth printing 1999

Printed in the United Kingdom at the University Press, Cambridge

ISBN 0 521 49900 3 Self-study edition ✓
ISBN 0 521 49899 6 Student's Book
ISBN 0 521 49901 1 Teacher's Book
ISBN 0 521 49902 X Cassette Set

Contents

Thanks

We are grateful to Jeanne McCarten, Elizabeth Sharman, Amanda Ogden, Judith Greet and Peter Ducker of CUP for their hard work in helping us; to everyone at AVP Recording Studio and to all the people at UCLES who provided us with information.

The authors and publishers would also like to thank the following people and institutions for piloting the material for us:

International House, Zaragoza; The Cheltenham School of English; Anna Bogobowicz, Warsaw; Eurocentres, Cambridge; The William Blake Institute, Buenos Aires.

Acknowledgements

The publishers are grateful to the following for permission to reproduce copyright material. It has not always been possible to identify sources of all the material used, and in such cases the publishers would welcome information from the copyright owners.

Focus magazine for the extracts on p.35 (*Focus* March 1995), on pp.66-67 (*Focus* July 1994), on pp.124-125 (*Focus* July 1994) and on p.54 (*Focus* May 1993); *The Observer* for the extract on pp.36-37 from 'The Summit of Self-Made Satisfaction' by Roger Smith (*The Observer* 30.5.96); *BBC Music Magazine* for the extract on pp.39-40 from 'Bell Epoque' by Lindsay Kemp (*BBC Music Magazine* December 1993); *National Magazine Company* for the extract on p.43 from 'Do women do it better?' by Gillian Fairchild (*Good Housekeeping* March 1993) and for the extract on p.97 from 'Guide to the guides' by James Daunt (*Country Living Traveller* February 1995); *The Radio Times* for the extract on pp.62-63 from 'My kind of day' by Colin Jackson (*Radio Times* 20-26 August 1994) and for the extract on pp.117-118 from 'Take One Novice' (*Radio Times* 10-16 September 1994); Nicola Upson for the extracts on pp.64-65 from 'Learning to play the piano' by Charlotte Cory (*Second Shift* Issue 4) and on pp.90-91 from 'Biologically correct' by Heather Angel (*Second Shift* Issue 4); *Mediawatch Ltd*, for the extract on p.69 (*Healthy Eating* March 1994); the extract on pp.88-89 is from *Which?* December 1991, published by Consumers' Association, 2 Marylebone Road, London NW1 4DF. To find out more, including how to get *Which?* free for 3 months, please write to Department A3, FREEPOST, Hertford SG14 1YB or telephone free on 0800 252100; *Financial Times* for the extract on pp.93-94 (*Financial Times* 19/20.11.94); *The Guardian* for the extract on p.116 from 'Unable to think about it' (*Education Guardian* 18.1.94); the extract on pp.120-121 is from World-Wide Research and Publishing Company's 'National Parkways, Yosemite National Park'; Jean Saunders and Donna Thompson for the extract on p.50 adapted from 'How to write a bestseller' (*Woman's Weekly* 30.8.94); *Wildlife Magazine* for the extract on p.74 adapted from 'The whatsit of Oz' by Richard Greenwell (*Wildlife Magazine* February 1994); *Kogan Page* Publishers for the extract on p.80 adapted from *Job Hunting for Women* (2nd ed.) by Margaret Wallis, published 1990 by *Kogan Page Ltd*, London; *IPC Magazines* for the extract on p.104 adapted from 'We're on the box – again!' by Nuala Duxbury (*Woman's Realm* 23.8.94); *Reed Books* for the extract on p.108 adapted from *The World of Toys* by J. Kandert (Octopus Illustrated Publishing); *Element Books Ltd* of Shaftesbury, Dorset for the extract on p.130 adapted from *The Elements of Visualisation* by Ursula Markham (*Element Books* 1989); Ray K. Kinross for the extract on p.132 adapted from 'Ice rage after ice age' by Felicity Kinross (*The Times Saturday Review* 17.8.1991); *Popular Crafts* Magazine for the extract on p.136 adapted from 'Making a living' (*Popular Crafts* April 1994); the answer sheets for Papers 1, 3 and 4 are reproduced by permission of the *University of Cambridge Local Examinations Syndicate*.

Photographs: Action-Plus/Tony Henshaw, p.62; Heather Angel, p.90; Harry Borden, p.39; Comstock Photo Library, p.120; Country Living/Wong Ling, p.97; Financial Times Pictures, p.93; The Hulton Deutsch Collection, p.88; Pictor International-London, p.66; Rex Features Ltd, pp.117, 124; Tony Stone Imges/Philip and Karen Smith, p.36.

Colour Paper 5 Section: Adams Picture Library, (2C); Gainsborough: Wooded Landscape, Christies, London/Bridgeman Art Library, London, (1A); British Telecommunications plc., (2E: telephone); The J. Allan Cash Photolibrary, (3E: bottom left); The Environmental Picture Library Ltd./Graham Burns, (3E: top, right); Chris Fairclough Colour Library, (3E: middle left); Hitachi Home Electronics (Europe) Ltd., (2E:television, radio-cassette player); Jeremy Pembrey, (1D, 2E: armchair, computer, bookshelves, 4E: top right, bottom); Performing Arts Library/Clive Barda, (4A); Pictor International-London, (3C, 4D); Redferns/Mick Hutson, (4B); Beth Gwinn/Retna Pictures Ltd., (4C); Tony Stone Images, (3D); Topham Picturepoint, (2A); Trip/Helene Rogers, (2D); Viewfinder Colour Photo Library, (2B, 3A); John Walmsley Photo Library, (3B, 4E: top left); Painting 'Shining Stream of Time' (1994) by Julius Tabacek (1B); Computer Art 'Life Study' (1992) by Abbas Hashemi (1C).

Picture research by Sandie Huskison-Rolfe (PHOTOSEEKERS)

Book design by Peter Ducker MSTD

Introduction

What is FCE?

The First Certificate in English (FCE) is an examination at intermediate level which is offered by UCLES (the University of Cambridge Local Examinations Syndicate). This book contains four practice tests which are very similar to the exam. You can use them to help you prepare for FCE. If you want more information about FCE and you cannot find it in this book, you should write to UCLES, 1 Hills Road, Cambridge CB1 2EU, England.

FCE consists of five papers, each carrying 20 per cent of the total marks.

Paper 1   Reading
You have 1 hour 15 minutes to answer the questions on the answer sheet provided. There are four parts, each containing a text and some questions. You are asked different kinds of questions in each part. There are 35 questions altogether.

Paper 2   Writing
You have 1 hour 30 minutes to write your answers on the answer sheet provided. You have to answer two questions. There is no choice in Part 1 but in Part 2 you can choose between four questions. One of these is about set books and you will only be able to answer this if you have prepared for it.

Paper 3   Use of English
You have 1 hour 15 minutes to answer the questions on the answer sheet provided. There are five different tasks which test your understanding and control of English grammar and vocabulary. There are 65 questions altogether.

Paper 4   Listening
You have 40 minutes to listen and answer the questions on the answer sheet provided. There are four parts – two parts contain long texts and the other two contain several short texts. You are asked different kinds of questions in each part. There are 30 questions altogether.

Paper 5   Speaking
The Speaking Test lasts for about 15 minutes. You take this test with another candidate. There are two examiners but only one takes part in the conversation with you. You will talk to the other candidate as well as to the examiner.

At the back of this book are examples of the answer sheets used in the exam.

When should I take the FCE exam?

If you already know something about Cambridge examinations, it is fairly easy to decide if you are ready for FCE. If you have passed the Preliminary English Test (PET), you will need about another 200 hours of active study, that is, about five hours a week for a year (either in a classroom or on your own) before you are ready to take FCE. This is an average and how long it takes you will depend on how hard you work, how quickly you learn, etc.

If you have not taken PET, look at Test 1 in this book. Try doing Paper 1 Part 2, Paper 3 Part 2 and Paper 4 Part 1. Check your answers in the Key. You need to average around 60 per cent across all five papers to be sure of passing FCE, although your score may be higher in some papers and lower in others.

Remember that FCE is not an elementary exam. If you are going to pass, you need to be fairly confident about English in all the following areas – reading, writing, listening, grammar, vocabulary and speaking. You need to be able to use and understand the main structures of English and a wide range of vocabulary and be able to communicate with English-speaking people in a range of social situations. People who pass FCE are usually considered to be ready to begin using English at work or for study.

What will I need in order to study for FCE?

You will need:
- A good English/English dictionary and a reliable modern reference grammar of English. There are excellent dictionaries and grammar reference books available which are specially written for students of English as a foreign language.
- A cassette recorder to play the cassettes which contain the listening tests. If you like music, you can use it to play songs in English on cassette and try listening to the words. Many cassettes and CDs have the words printed with them so you can look at the words while listening. You can also buy recordings of books on cassette read by famous actors.

You will find useful:
- An up-to-date translating dictionary (English/your language).
- A radio to listen to English-language programmes. For details of British overseas broadcasts, write to The BBC, Bush House, PO Box 76, The Strand, London WC2 4PH. Ask about programmes aimed at people studying English, as well as the usual programmes. It may also be possible to hear American or Australian radio stations in your area. Go to the local library or contact the local Consulates of English-speaking countries to find out.
- A video recorder so that you can watch English language films.
- English-speaking friends to practise with. Make the most of any chance to talk to people whose first language is English, but it is also very helpful to speak English with your friends. Remember, most people who learn English use it to communicate with other people who are also learners.
- An English-speaking penfriend. If you cannot find a penfriend whose first language is English, try exchanging letters in English with friends who may be studying English in another town.

- Magazines, newspapers and stories in English if you can find them. There are also series of simplified readers specially written for foreign learners which will help you improve your reading and vocabulary.

How should I organise my studying?

- Be realistic. Don't plan to do more than you can, you will only disappoint yourself.
- Don't plan to give up all your free time to studying. Studying hard for one hour four times a week can be very effective. In fact, short sessions are best, because your memory won't get tired, and so you will remember what you study.
- Try to study in a quiet place so that you can concentrate well.
- Be organised. Write out a timetable and follow it. Spend a few minutes of each study period revising what you did last time.

What does this book contain?

This book is divided into four parts:

Study notes
This part goes through each paper, explaining and describing the different questions. There are suggestions about how to answer the questions and how to prepare for the exam.

Taking the exam
This part contains practical information and advice about taking the exam.

The Practice Tests
This part contains the practice papers, which are like the real ones in the exam. There are four practice tests, each one containing five papers (Reading, Writing, Use of English, Listening, Speaking) as in the exam.

The Keys and Tapescripts
This part contains all the answers to the tests and the complete tapescript for the listening papers. For Paper 2 (Writing) there are example composition answers for Test 1 and example composition plans for Tests 2, 3 and 4.

Study notes

Paper 1 Reading

- The texts on Paper 1 come from a range of English-language publications – newspapers, magazines, stories, leaflets, instructions, advertisements. Try to read as much as you can in English so you get used to texts of different kinds.
- There are always four texts. At first it may seem that there is a lot to read but, when you look at the questions, you will realise that you do not need to understand every word.
- You can get an idea of what a text is going to be about by looking at the way it is laid out on the page, the way it is printed, the headings and any illustrations. These things will all help you when you start to read the text.
- Before you begin to answer the questions, always read the instructions carefully. Each part of the test asks you to do something different so make sure you have understood **all** the instructions before you begin. This book will give you practice in the reading tasks you may meet in the exam.
- Look at the examples in Parts 1, 3 and 4 where you are shown what to do.
- If you don't understand part of a text or a particular word, try to guess by looking at the words around it, but don't spend too long on it. Leave it and come back to it later as you may find it easier to understand when you have read the rest of the text. Remember you may not even need to understand it to answer the questions.
- Practise doing the paper in the time allowed so you do not need to rush any parts in the exam.
- Practise transferring your answers to the answer sheet. In the exam, it is better to do this while you are doing the test rather than leave it till the end. If you don't do this, you might run out of time, and have no answers to hand in. If you don't know, always guess – you may be right!

Part 1

Part 1 is always a matching exercise – matching paragraphs in a text to either summary sentences (see below) or headings (e.g. Test 2 Part 1). The example below is a summary sentences exercise. The paragraphs in the text are numbered **1–6**. There are always six or seven questions plus the example. The first paragraph is the example (0) and is done for you. The headings or summary sentences appear in a box before the text and each one has a letter (**A–H**). The last letter is always the answer to the example. There is always one extra heading or summary sentence which does not fit anywhere.

- Read the summary sentences first. Then read the text through once. Now go back to the beginning and, after you have read each paragraph, try to match it with its summary sentence. If you are not sure, leave a blank or put a question mark on your question paper.
- If you think two answers fit one question, note them both on the question paper. When you have finished, go back to the beginning and read the text again, this time choosing and checking your final answers. Then transfer them to the answer sheet.

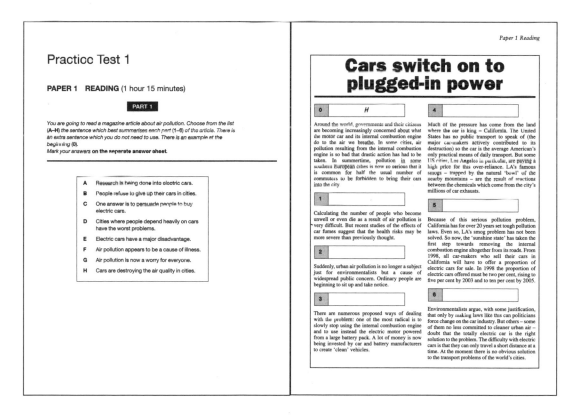

Practice Test 1

PAPER 1   READING (1 hour 15 minutes)

PART 1

You are going to read a magazine article about air pollution. Choose from the list (A–H) the sentence which best summarises each part (1–6) of the article. There is an extra sentence which you do not need to use. There is an example at the beginning (0).
Mark your answers on the separate answer sheet.

A	Research is being done into electric cars.
B	People refuse to give up their cars in cities.
C	One answer is to persuade people to buy electric cars.
D	Cities where people depend heavily on cars have the worst problems.
E	Electric cars have a major disadvantage.
F	Air pollution appears to be a cause of illness.
G	Air pollution is now a worry for everyone.
H	Cars are destroying the air quality in cities.

Paper 1 Reading

Cars switch on to plugged-in power

0   *H*

Around the world, governments and their citizens are becoming increasingly concerned about what the motor car and its internal combustion engine do to the air we breathe. In some cities, air pollution resulting from the internal combustion engine is so bad that drastic action has had to be taken. In summertime, pollution in some southern European cities is now so serious that it is common for half the usual number of commuters to be forbidden to bring their cars into the city.

1

Calculating the number of people who become unwell or even die as a result of air pollution is very difficult. But recent studies of the effects of car fumes suggest that the health risks may be more severe than previously thought.

2

Suddenly, urban air pollution is no longer a subject just for environmentalists but a cause of widespread public concern. Ordinary people are beginning to sit up and take notice.

3

There are numerous proposed ways of dealing with the problem: one of the most radical is to slowly stop using the internal combustion engine and to use instead the electric motor powered from a large battery pack. A lot of money is now being invested by car and battery manufacturers to create 'clean' vehicles.

4

Much of the pressure has come from the land where the car is king – California. The United States has no public transport to speak of (the major car-makers actively contributed to its destruction) so the car is the average American's only practical means of daily transport. But some US cities, Los Angeles in particular, are paying a high price for this over-reliance. LA's famous smogs – trapped by the natural 'bowl' of the nearby mountains – are the result of reactions between the chemicals which come from the city's millions of car exhausts.

5

Because of this serious pollution problem, California has for over 20 years set tough pollution laws. Even so, LA's smog problem has not been solved. So now, the 'sunshine state' has taken the first step towards removing the internal combustion engine altogether from its roads. From 1998, all car-makers who sell their cars in California will have to offer a proportion of electric cars for sale. In 1998 the proportion of electric cars offered must be two per cent, rising to five per cent by 2003 and to ten per cent by 2005.

6

Environmentalists argue, with some justification, that only by making laws like this can politicians force change on the car industry. But others – some of them no less committed to cleaner urban air – doubt that the totally electric car is the right solution to the problem. The difficulty with electric cars is that they can only travel a short distance at a time. At the moment there is no obvious solution to the transport problems of the world's cities.

Part 2

PART 2

You are going to read an article about a photographer. For questions 7–14, choose the answer (A, B, C or D) which you think fits best according to the text. Mark your answers on the separate answer sheet.

Biologically Correct

MY LOVE OF NATURE goes right back to my childhood, to the times when I stayed on my grandparents' farm in Suffolk. My father was in the armed forces, so we were always moving and didn't have a home base for any length of time, but I loved going there. I think it was my grandmother who encouraged me more than anyone: she taught me the names of wildflowers and got me interested in looking at the countryside, so it seemed obvious to me to do Zoology at university.

I didn't get my first camera until after I'd graduated, when I was due to go diving in Norway and needed a method of recording the sea creatures I would find there. My father didn't know anything about photography, but he bought me an Exacta, which was really quite a good camera for the time, and I went off to take my first pictures of sea anemones and starfish. I became keen very quickly, and learned how to develop and print; obviously I didn't have much money in those days, so I did more black-and-white photography than colour, but it was all still using the camera very much as a tool to record what I found both by diving and on the shore. I had no ambition at all to be a photographer then, or even for some years afterwards.

Unlike many of the wildlife photographers of the time, I trained as a scientist and therefore my way of expressing myself is very different. I've tried from the beginning to produce pictures which are always biologically correct. There are people who will alter things deliberately: you don't pick up sea creatures from the middle of the shore and take them down to attractive pools at the bottom of the shore without knowing you're doing it. In so doing you're actually falsifying the sort of seaweeds they live on and so on, which may seem unimportant but it is actually changing the natural surroundings to make them prettier. Unfortunately, many of the people who select pictures are looking for attractive images and, at the end of the day, whether it's truthful or not doesn't really matter to them.

It's important to think about the animal first, and there are many occasions when I've not taken a picture because it would have been too disturbing. Nothing is so important that you have to get that shot; of course, there are cases when it would be very sad if you didn't, but it's not the end of the world. There can be a lot of ignorance in people's behaviour towards wild animals and it's a problem that more and more people are going to wild places: while some animals may get used to cars, they won't get used to people suddenly rushing up to them. The sheer pressure of people, coupled with the fact that there are increasingly few places where no-one else has photographed, means that over the years, life has become much more difficult for the professional wildlife photographer.

Nevertheless, wildlife photographs play a very important part in educating people about what is out there and what needs conserving. Although photography can be an enjoyable pastime, as it is to many people, it is also something that plays a very important part in educating young and old alike. Of the qualities it takes to make a good wildlife photographer, patience is perhaps the most obvious – you just have to be prepared to sit it out. I'm actually more patient now because I write more than ever before, and as long as I've got a bit of paper and a pencil, I don't feel I'm wasting my time. And because I photograph such a wide range of things, even if the main target doesn't appear I can probably find something else to concentrate on instead.

7 Heather Angel decided to go to university and study Zoology because
 A she wanted to improve her life in the countryside.
 B she was persuaded to do so by her grandmother.
 C she was keen on the natural world.
 D she wanted to stop moving around all the time.

8 Why did she get her first camera?
 A She needed to be able to look back at what she had seen.
 B She wanted to find out if she enjoyed photography.
 C Her father thought it was a good idea for her to have one.
 D She wanted to learn how to use one and develop her own prints.

9 How is she different from some of the other wildlife photographers she meets?
 A She tries to make her photographs as attractive as possible.
 B She takes photographs which record accurate natural conditions.
 C She likes to photograph plants as well as wildlife.
 D She knows the best places to find wildlife.

This is always a multiple choice exercise – there are seven or eight questions which have four-choice answers. You must choose **A, B, C** or **D** as the correct answer.

- Read the text first. Try to get a general idea of what it is about. Try to understand as much as possible of the detail while you are reading but, if there are parts you do not understand, do not spend lots of time on them as they may not be tested.
- Look at the first question and find the part of the text which it refers to. Read that section again and answer the question. Only one of the choices is correct.
- Most of the questions test detailed understanding of the text but one or two test whether you understand the relation between words and phrases in one part of the text. For example, to answer question 10 alongside, find the word 'them' and

10 What does 'them' refer to in line 45?
 A sea creatures
 B attractive pools
 C seaweeds
 D natural surroundings

11 Heather Angel now finds it more difficult to photograph wild animals because
 A there are fewer of them.
 B they have become more nervous of people.
 C it is harder to find suitable places.
 D they have become frightened of cars.

12 Wildlife photography is important because it can make people realise that
 A photography is an enjoyable hobby.
 B we learn little about wildlife at school.
 C it is worthwhile visiting the countryside.
 D it is important to look after wild animals.

13 Why is she more patient now?
 A She does other things while waiting.
 B She has got used to waiting.
 C She can concentrate better than she used to.
 D She knows the result will be worth it.

14 Which of the following describes Heather Angel?
 A proud
 B sensitive
 C aggressive
 D disappointed

read the text around it (several sentences) to decide exactly what it refers to.

- The questions all come in the order of the information in the text but one question (usually the last) may test your understanding of the complete text, e.g. question 14.
- When you have finished, transfer your answers to the answer sheet.

Part 3

This is always a gapped text – either gapped sentences or gapped paragraphs.

There are six or seven questions plus an example. In a gapped sentence exercise, one sentence has been removed from every paragraph of a text and you have to fit them back where they belong (e.g. Test 2, Part 3).

In a gapped paragraph exercise, a number of paragraphs have been removed from a text and you have to fit them back where they belong (see below).

The sentences or paragraphs which have been removed are in a box which comes after the text. Each gap in the text has a number (**1, 2, 3**, etc.) and each sentence/paragraph in the box has a letter (**A, B, C,** etc.). The first gap in the text is labelled **0** and is the example, so it is done for you. There is one extra sentence/paragraph in the box, which does not fit anywhere.

- Read through the main text to get a general idea of what it is saying.
- Then read the sentences/paragraphs in the box. Notice anything about them which makes them different from each other, e.g. some may be in the past tense, some in the present tense.

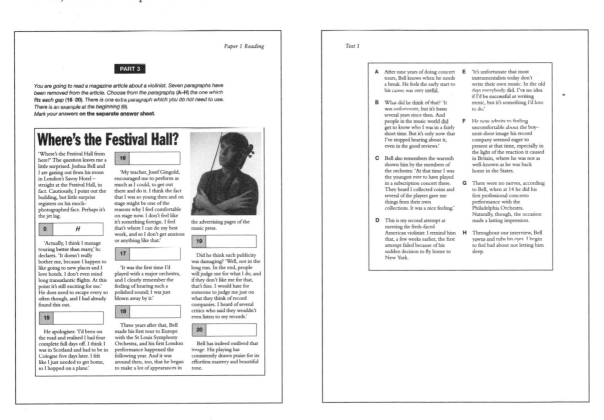

- Go back to the text and look at the first gap. Look at the sentences before and after the gap and decide what information is needed to join them together. Now look at the sentences/paragraphs in the box again and try to find the one which fits. If you can't decide, leave that one and come back to it later as some of the other gaps may be easier.
- When you are happy with your answers, transfer them to the answer sheet.

Part 4

This is always a multiple matching exercise with between 13 and 15 questions. You are asked to find different pieces of information in the text. There may also be a multiple choice question at the end which tests your understanding of the text as a whole. Part 4 may look harder than some of the other parts of the paper because there are so many questions but they are usually quicker to do

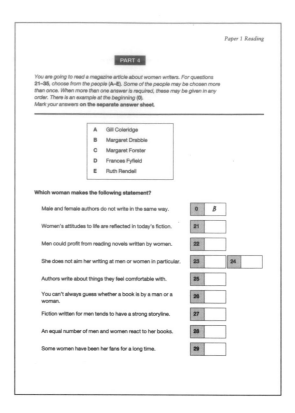

Paper 1 Reading

PART 4

You are going to read a magazine article about women writers. For questions 21–35, choose from the people (A–E). Some of the people may be chosen more than once. When more than one answer is required, these may be given in any order. There is an example at the beginning (0).
Mark your answers **on the separate answer sheet.**

A	Gill Coleridge
B	Margaret Drabble
C	Margaret Forster
D	Frances Fyfield
E	Ruth Rendell

Which woman makes the following statement?

Male and female authors do not write in the same way.	0	*B*
Women's attitudes to life are reflected in today's fiction.	21	
Men could profit from reading novels written by women.	22	
She does not aim her writing at men or women in particular.	23	24
Authors write about things they feel comfortable with.	25	
You can't always guess whether a book is by a man or a woman.	26	
Fiction written for men tends to have a strong storyline.	27	
An equal number of men and women react to her books.	28	
Some women have been her fans for a long time.	29	

She aims her writing mainly at women.	30
She doesn't change her writing because of what other people might think.	31
Women readers like to get emotionally involved with the characters in a novel.	32
Her main aim is for her books to be interesting.	33
Authors who want financial success aim at a particular type of reader.	34
Women like reading about other women who lead more fulfilled lives.	35

Is what we believe about women writers fact or fiction?

Women read more than men: that's official. And statistically, what do they like reading best? Novels. Novels about love, novels about crime, novels that are funny, clever and deep but above all, novels written by other women.

There is, of course, an enormous difference between 'popular' and 'literary' fiction. As literary agent **Gill Coleridge** explains, 'In the commercial side of the business, the most important feature of male fiction is the plot, whereas in female fiction it is characters that the reader can identify with and care about. Commercial authors focus on a chosen audience, writers of literary novels write what they want to say.'

Margaret Drabble, who has written several successful literary novels, says that she never imagines her reader to be male or female when she sits down to write. 'That person changes from chapter to chapter. Sometimes I think about friends – I bet Judith would like this or James would hate that, but it doesn't affect what I write. There's

been a change in the last two or three decades in how a whole generation of women look at the world and therefore what they accept in their fiction. Luckily for me, a fairly loyal readership of women has grown old along with me, taken the same journey. But because men and women react differently to things, there is a difference in how male and female authors write. We tend to write about things we like and which are sympathetic to us.' She claims to be much more aware now of the male reader, because the different worlds which men and women live in are less separate nowadays than they used to be.

As a novelist and biographer (she has written the life stories of several well-known people), **Margaret Forster** says of the letters she receives from readers that men and women write to her in equal numbers. Of women readers she says, 'Women are hungry for details of other people's lives, particularly women's lives: biography as well as fiction provides that second-hand

experience. Many women get to middle age and wonder where their life has gone, why they haven't made more of it: reading about others who have achieved something enlarges their vision.'

Crime writer **Frances Fyfield** wishes that more men would read more fiction, especially by women. 'If all you read is thrillers and adventures, you're bound to have a gap of knowledge. I write very much with the female reader in mind, though I take my male readers into account too.'

Crime writer **Ruth Rendell** says she cannot always tell male writing from female writing: 'Women are always credited with being better at writing detail, men with taking the wider view. But I've just been rereading Anthony Powell's *A Dance To The Music Of Time* and it's full of detail. Just as many men as women read my books. I don't think of my audience as being one or the other, only that there shouldn't be too many things that they find dull.'

than multiple choice or gapped text questions. The text may also look long but you do not usually need to understand every word.

- Read the questions first and then look through the text trying to find the answers. You do not need to understand every word. When you have found the answer, note it down. If you are unsure, put a question mark beside it so that you can go back and check it later when you have done the other questions and know the text better.
- Transfer your answers to the answer sheet.

Paper 2 Writing

- Each of your answers must be between 120 and 180 words. The exact number is not important. The best thing to do is to measure your handwriting when you are preparing for the exam, so that you know what 120 and 180 words in your writing look like. Once you know, you can avoid wasting valuable time counting words during the actual exam.

- The examiners do not expect your work to be perfect. Even the best students make some mistakes when they write. However, you want to make as few as possible. While you are practising for the exam, it may help you to know that you can lose marks for the following:
  - including inappropriate details (especially in Part 1)
  - using material from the exam paper without adapting it to fit what you are writing (especially in Part 1)
  - leaving out important information
  - work which is not clearly organised (for example, giving information in the wrong order)
  - incorrect style (for example, writing a job application as if you were talking to a friend)
  - incorrect grammar (especially repeated mistakes or mistakes that affect meaning such as verb tenses)
  - bad spelling
  - bad punctuation
  - bad paragraphing
  - illegible handwriting

Try to set out your work tidily. If you need to change what you have written, cross out the wrong words with a single line. Do not use brackets ( ) for this.

Part 1

In Part 1, there is no choice. Everyone has to do the same task, and it is always a letter. It will not be a very formal business letter, but if it is addressed to someone you do not know very well, or a stranger, it should not sound like a letter to a friend. On the exam paper you will see up to three short texts such as advertisements, letters, notes, leaflets, diaries, timetables, notices. These texts contain all the information you need for your letter. You must read the instructions and these texts very carefully.

- Check **who** you have to write to, **why** you are writing and **what** you must include. This will help you to choose the right style, include everything you should, and avoid adding unnecessary information. You can add ideas of your own as well, provided they fit sensibly with those in the text. It is useful to mark the exam paper with a pen or highlighter so that you can see which information is important.

- Then you should make a short plan (see examples on page 144). This is very important. If you have already put your ideas in order before you begin to write, you can think carefully about your language and avoid mistakes.

- It is not a good idea to copy out whole sentences from the texts on the question paper. Of course, you may need to use some of the same words and phrases, but you must take care that they fit the meaning, and grammar of what you are writing (see model answer on page 144).

- You do not have to include any addresses, but you should begin and end in a suitable way.

Part 2

In Part 2, there are five tasks, from which you choose **only one**. The two choices in question 5 are related to the set books (see below). Do not attempt to answer the set book questions in the exam if you have not prepared for them. The other tasks always include at least one letter, report or application and at least one description or story or discussion.

- In every case you are told **what** to write (letter, story, etc.) and for **whom** you are writing, but in this part, it is up to you to decide on the details of the contents. Be careful to follow the instructions exactly. If you are given words for the beginning of a story, do not change them, or put them in the middle! If you are asked to write a report, this does not have to be a very formal business report. Just make sure that you think carefully about who is going to

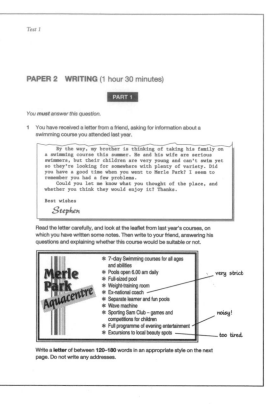

read it and what they want to learn from it. Include only the sort of information and opinions that are asked for. The tasks are always different in Parts 1 and 2, so even if you write two letters, they will be quite different types.

- Again, it is very important to make a plan. As well as helping you to write correct English, it will also allow you to discover in time if you have chosen the wrong task for you. For example, you may realise that you do not remember some essential vocabulary, or that you do not have enough ideas to write about. You can quickly choose another one before you have wasted too much time.

Using the Practice Tests for Paper 2

In the Key, you will find plans for the Part 1 and Part 2 tasks of Practice Test 1. These are to help you judge the sort of thing you should write and how to organise it.

First stage (Practice Test 1)

- check exactly what you have to do (**who** are you writing to? **why** are you writing?)
- mark the important parts of the task
- write a plan
- compare your plan with the one in the Key
- make any changes you want to (remember, your plan may work just as well, so only make changes if there is a clear need to do so)
- write your answer (try to do this in about 30 minutes)
- read your answer through carefully, looking for mistakes
- compare your answer with the model – what can you learn from it? (remember, your answer may be very good, even though it is not the same)

Second stage (Practice Tests 2, 3 and 4)

- check exactly what you have to do
- mark the important parts of the task
- write a plan
- write your answer (try to do this in about 30 minutes)
- read your answer through carefully, looking for mistakes
- (for Part 1) compare your answer with the plan in the Key – what can you learn from it? (remember, your answer may be very good, even though it is not the same)

The set book questions

In Part 2 of Paper 2, there is a pair of questions about set books. If you have read any of the set books, you may choose to do **one** of these **instead of** the other questions in Part 2. The books change every two years. To find out which titles are set when you are taking the exam, look in the regulations booklet or write to UCLES (see page 1).

You do not have to read the set books, but it can be a good idea to do so. There are several reasons for this:

- Reading will help your English in general.
- It increases your choices in Paper 2 Part 2, especially if you read more than one of the books.
- It allows you to write about a subject which you know well.

Preparation

If you study the questions about set books in this book, you will see that they are always general questions which can be answered about any of the books.

- Practise describing and giving your opinion about the characters, events and settings of the books.
- Plan and check your work just as with other writing tasks.
- Do not worry about giving correct 'literary' opinions. The examiners who mark your paper are not really concerned about how clever your ideas are. They want to know how well you can use the English language to express yourself.
- Make sure that you really know the book well, so that you can answer any question about it.
- Do **not** prepare 'perfect' answers and try to fit them to any question. Examiners are very strict if they think they are marking an inappropriate answer which has been 'prepared' before the exam.

Paper 3 Use of English

- Try to spend approximately the same amount of time on each part of the paper, with probably a little more on Part 3, and a little less on Part 5. It is also important to allow enough time to check your answers, and your answer sheet, carefully.
- If you have large, and/or untidy, handwriting, you will need to be very careful when completing the answer sheet, especially in Part 3. Be very careful with your spelling in all parts of the paper.
- When the task is based on a text (Parts 1, 2, 4 and 5), read quickly through the text before you try to answer any of the questions. Don't miss out the 'example' sentences at the beginning, which will help you to get a quick general idea of what the text is about.
- The texts for Paper 3 are not as long, or as complicated, as the texts in the Reading Paper, but you should still read them carefully, to avoid losing marks through misunderstanding.
- **Parts 1, 2, 3** and **5** are all gap-filling exercises and have many similarities in the way you should work on them. Remember these points:
  - Most of the information which will help you to make the correct answer will be in the areas immediately before **or after** the gap. Everyone looks before the gap, but lots of students miss what comes after (e.g. *interested* is usually followed by *in* and so it wouldn't be a good choice as an answer to '(18) ... for').
  - If you have a problem with some of the questions on a text, try not to waste time. Go on and do the easier questions, and come back to the difficult ones later. It's often simpler to find an answer when you have completed most of the text.

- If you have time, it is a good idea to read through the completed text to make sure that all your answers make sense. A few answers may be affected by ideas which are not close to the gap, and you might miss these when you are working question by question. If you do not have time to check like this when you start preparing for the exam, then you should try to improve your working speed gradually.

Part 1

Part 1 is a text of around 200 words with fifteen gaps in it. You have to choose the correct answer from four options to fill each of the gaps. The questions test mainly vocabulary.

- In most of the questions, you have to choose the only answer with the correct meaning for the gap. In a few questions, however, two or more choices may have the right meaning, and you will have to choose the only one that fits the grammar of the text.
- Some of the questions are based on fixed phrases, so it is a good idea to make a careful note of these as you meet them in your reading.

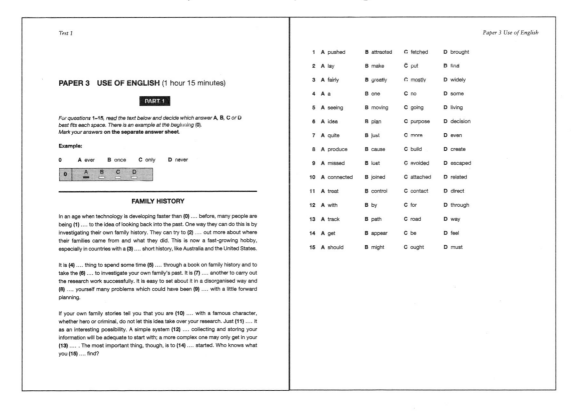

Test 1

Paper 3 Use of English

PAPER 3   USE OF ENGLISH (1 hour 15 minutes)

PART 1

*For questions 1–15, read the text below and decide which answer **A, B, C** or **D** best fits each space. There is an example at the beginning (0).*
*Mark your answers **on the separate answer sheet**.*

Example:

0   **A** ever   **B** once   **C** only   **D** never

0   A   B   C   D

FAMILY HISTORY

In an age when technology is developing faster than **(0)** .... before, many people are being **(1)** .... to the idea of looking back into the past. One way they can do this is by investigating their own family history. They can try to **(2)** .... out more about where their families came from and what they did. This is now a fast-growing hobby, especially in countries with a **(3)** .... short history, like Australia and the United States.

It is **(4)** .... thing to spend some time **(5)** .... through a book on family history and to take the **(6)** .... to investigate your own family's past. It is **(7)** .... another to carry out the research work successfully. It is easy to set about it in a disorganised way and **(8)** .... yourself many problems which could have been **(9)** .... with a little forward planning.

If your own family stories tell you that you are **(10)** .... with a famous character, whether hero or criminal, do not let this idea take over your research. Just **(11)** .... it as an interesting possibility. A simple system **(12)** .... collecting and storing your information will be adequate to start with; a more complex one may only get in your **(13)** .... . The most important thing, though, is to **(14)** .... started. Who knows what you **(15)** .... find?

1	**A** pushed	**B** attracted	**C** fetched	**D** brought
2	**A** lay	**B** make	**C** put	**D** find
3	**A** fairly	**B** greatly	**C** mostly	**D** widely
4	**A** a	**B** one	**C** no	**D** some
5	**A** seeing	**B** moving	**C** going	**D** living
6	**A** idea	**B** plan	**C** purpose	**D** decision
7	**A** quite	**B** just	**C** more	**D** even
8	**A** produce	**B** cause	**C** build	**D** create
9	**A** missed	**B** lost	**C** avoided	**D** escaped
10	**A** connected	**B** joined	**C** attached	**D** related
11	**A** treat	**B** control	**C** contact	**D** direct
12	**A** with	**B** by	**C** for	**D** through
13	**A** track	**B** path	**C** road	**D** way
14	**A** get	**B** appear	**C** be	**D** feel
15	**A** should	**B** might	**C** ought	**D** must

Part 2

Part 2 is also a text of around 200 words with fifteen gaps in it. This time you have to decide on the best word to fill each gap for yourself: there are no options to choose from. You must use **only one word** in each gap. For example, *close to* may have the correct meaning to fill a particular gap, but has too many words: *near* would be the correct choice. These questions concentrate on your knowledge of English grammar, and the words you need to fill the gaps will be quite familiar.

- When you have finished, be careful to check, for example, that singulars and plurals match up correctly, that all the verb tenses work properly, and that longer sentences are properly connected, and have a clear meaning.
- If you have trouble with a gap, try to decide what part of speech you need (e.g. noun, verb, pronoun, etc.), so that you can see how the sentence works. This may help with the next question, even if you don't find the exact word. Some questions may have more than one correct answer, but these will usually have the same meaning (e.g. *each/every*; *because/as/since*). You will get to know most of these groups as you practise for the examination. Above all, try not to waste time choosing the best of two or three equally correct answers.

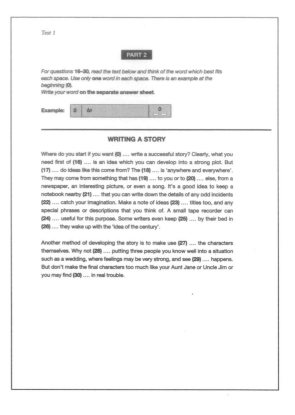

Part 3

Part 3 consists of ten separate questions, which test both grammar and vocabulary. You have to complete a gap in a sentence so that it means the same as the sentence printed above it. You are given one 'key' word which you must use as part of the answer. You must not change this word in any way, and your answer must contain **a minimum of two words and a maximum of five,** including the key word. As in Part 2, you may be able to think of a longer way of filling the gap with correct English, but **answers of six words and more will lose marks,** so you must follow the rules very carefully.

- Read the original sentence very carefully, and notice which parts of the meaning are missing from the new sentence (your answer must not lose any important parts of the meaning of the original sentence). Then, look at the key word and think what else will be necessary when you fit it into the gap, perhaps a verb or noun will need to be followed by a particular preposition, or an infinitive may need other suitable words to form the correct tense. Be especially careful if the key word could be two different parts of speech (e.g. *help* – noun and verb; *good* – adjective and noun), since it is likely that only one of these will make a successful answer.
- It is fine to use **short forms** (e.g. *you're, won't, we've, they'd*, etc.) in your answers, but **you must count them as two words,** since that is what they represent (e.g. *you are, will not, we have, they would*, etc.). Apostrophes ('), of

course, can also show possession – in phrases like *David's house, the policeman's car,* etc. In this case, *David's* and *policeman's* count as **one word** each.

- Do not change any vocabulary from the original sentence unless the question forces you to do this. It may seem safe to change *able* to *capable,* even though you do not have to, but there is no point in doing this, and it may lead to other problems which you haven't noticed.
- Check that your answer does not unnecessarily repeat ideas which are already in the new sentence, and remember: answers which change the key word in any way or use too many words will lose marks.
- As you work through the Practice Tests, notice the points which are commonly tested, so that you have an idea of what to expect in the examination. When you are studying grammar, look out for any exercises which ask you to express the same idea in different ways.

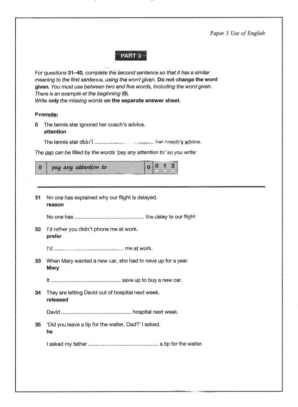

Paper 3 Use of English

PART 3

For questions 31–40, complete the second sentence so that it has a similar meaning to the first sentence, using the word given. Do not change the word given. You must use between two and five words, including the word given. There is an example at the beginning (0).
Write only the missing words on the separate answer sheet.

Example:

0   The tennis star ignored her coach's advice.
attention

The tennis star didn't .... her coach's advice.

The gap can be filled by the words 'pay any attention to' so you write:

0	pay any attention to		0 0 1 2

31   No one has explained why our flight is delayed.
reason

No one has .... the delay to our flight.

32   I'd rather you didn't phone me at work.
prefer

I'd .... me at work.

33   When Mary wanted a new car, she had to save up for a year.
Mary

It .... save up to buy a new car.

34   They are letting David out of hospital next week.
released

David .... hospital next week.

35   'Did you leave a tip for the waiter, Dad?' I asked.
he

I asked my father .... a tip for the waiter.

Test 1

36   Jane didn't expect to win the competition, but she entered it anyway.
went

Jane didn't expect to win the competition, but she .... it anyway.

37   I do not intend to tell you my plans.
intention

I .... you my plans.

38   Don't sign for the parcel until you have checked that everything is there.
you

Make sure that nothing is .... sign for the parcel.

39   Sasha only moved to a new class because her teacher recommended it.
Sasha

If her teacher hadn't recommended it, ... to a new class.

40   The motor in this machine needs cleaning once a week.
has

The motor in this machine .... once a week.

Part 4

Part 4 is a text of about 200 words with mistakes in most of the lines. You have to tick (✓) correct lines and for incorrect lines, you must write the *extra and unnecessary* word which makes the line incorrect in the space provided on your answer sheet. This exercise tests your ability to notice a variety of errors in a piece of connected English.

- Although not all the mistakes will be the type you make in your own writing, practising checking English for errors will help you in your own work for the Writing paper. If you have the opportunity, exchange written work with a friend. This can provide variety, and it is often easier to learn to notice mistakes in someone else's work, rather than your own.

- Between three and five of the fifteen tested lines will be correct. The extra words which you must find are always clearly inappropriate, not just words which can be left out, and these errors may appear anywhere in the line. This means that a word early in the line may be wrong because of something in the line above; a word near the end may be wrong because of what follows on the next line. For this reason, it is important to remember that you are working on a **complete** text, and not fifteen separate questions.

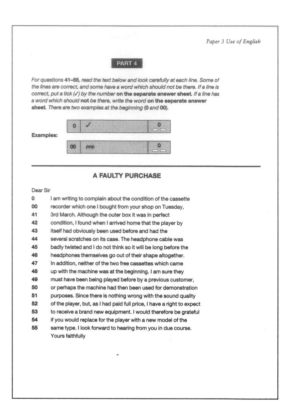

Part 5

Part 5 is a text of about 150 words with ten gaps in it. You have to fill the gaps by forming suitable parts of speech from the words given in capitals at the side of each line. You may, for example, have to turn a verb into a noun (e.g. *appear → appearance*), a noun into an adverb (e.g. *success → successfully*), etc. These questions test your ability to decide which part of speech is needed and to form the correct answer.

- You may have to think about other ideas in the text to find the right answer. For example, whether a person in a text is *fortunate* or *unfortunate* may depend on ideas which are some distance from the gap you are working on.
- When you have to form a noun, check the text carefully to see whether you need a singular or plural. If you write *argument*, and the text needs *arguments*, you will not get a mark.

- No correct answer will involve making more than two changes to the original word given (e.g. *interest* → **uninterested** may be included, *interest* → **uninterestedly** will not be).
- If you have not taken an interest in word groups so far, now is the time to start. You may need to change the way you collect and store your vocabulary. When looking up new words in the dictionary, it is worth taking a little extra time to note down the noun that goes with a new verb and so on. You can also find useful exercises on prefixes and suffixes in many intermediate grammar books.

Paper 4 Listening

- The best preparation for the Listening paper is listening to a wide variety of spoken English. You should listen to English as often as you can, in any form available, both in school and outside. If you are not in an English-speaking country, try to get information about English language broadcasts on the radio or television. You should also look out for recorded material such as audio cassettes of songs and videos of films in English. It does not matter whether these use British or American English or what sort of accents the speakers have. The important thing is to get used to listening to spoken English. Some of the accents in the FCE examination are not standard British English, although they will never be very strong.
- Remember that these Practice Tests are at the level of difficulty of the exam. Do not start using them too early, or you may be discouraged because they seem difficult. Wait until you have had lots of listening practice with other materials and then use these Practice Tests to help you get to know what it is like to do the Listening paper.
- When you are using these Practice Tests, it is better to practise as if you were in an exam. Do not keep stopping and rewinding the tape while you are trying to answer the questions. Get used to doing each whole test without interruptions because this is what you will have to do in the exam. After you've completed and marked your test using the Key, then is the time to listen again, and look at the tapescript if you like, to help with the questions that gave you problems.
- At the end of the test you have five minutes to copy your answers onto the answer sheet. It is very important to do this carefully, checking that you do not put any answers next to the wrong question number. Also be sure you do not leave any blanks. You cannot score marks for a blank space, but a guess may be correct.

Part 1

In Part 1 there are eight questions. For each one, you hear one or two people talking for about thirty seconds. You hear this twice and have to choose the best answer **A**, **B** or **C**. The questions are read out on the tape as well, so you will not lose your place.

- Practise using the questions to help you. Do not worry about understanding every word, just listen for the information you need. Sometimes you need understand only the words used. At other times a tone of voice or emphasis may be just as important.

- Be careful with those questions in which people develop an idea or change their minds as they speak.

PAPER 4 LISTENING (approximately 40 minutes)

PART 1

You will hear people talking in eight different situations.
For questions 1–8, choose the best answer A, B or C.

1 You hear someone introducing a programme on the radio. Where is he?

   A a swimming pool

   B a sports hall   1

   C a football ground

2 You hear this girl talking to her mother. What plan had her mother agreed to?

   A visiting a friend

   B going to London   2

   C staying in a hotel

3 You hear this advertisement for a concert. What is unusual about it?

   A It's on...

Part 2

In Part 2 you hear one or two people talking for about three minutes. You have to answer ten questions by writing one or a few words. You **never** have to write a whole sentence. You have time to read through the questions before the piece begins, there is a short pause after you hear it and then it is repeated.

Paper 4 Listening

PART 2

You will hear two radio presenters talking about some of the programmes for the coming month.
For questions 9–18, complete the information. You will need to write a word or a short phrase.

Monday 6th
Elton John talking about his   9

Wednesday 8th
Win a prize by guessing name of the   10

Thursday 9th
Sez U's visit to   11

- You can write your answers at any time. Spelling mistakes do not lose marks, as long as the examiners can understand what you mean.
- Read the questions carefully because they will help you to understand what you hear. For example, in question 9 you can think about the things Elton John might talk about, such as his music, his work or his career. If you have thought about possible answers, it will be easier to spot the correct one when you are listening.

Part 3

In Part 3 there are five questions. You hear five pieces of speech, each about thirty seconds in length. On your question paper there is a list of six possible answers which you must match against the five pieces you hear. The group of five pieces is repeated.

- Again, use the questions to help you. Notice whether the questions are about **what** the speakers say, **who** they are, **how** they feel, etc., because you will need to listen for different types of clue in each case.

Test 1

PART 3

You will hear five people talking about the jobs they'd like to have.
For questions 19–23, choose from the list A–F what they describe. Use the letters only once. There is one extra letter which you do not need to use.

This person would like to be:

A a journalist

B a hotel receptionist   Speaker 1   19

C a garden designer   Speaker 2   20

                                          Speaker 3   21

D a nurse   Speaker 4   22

                                          Speaker 5   23

E a chemist

- Use the first listening to form a general idea of the answers, but try to keep an open mind until you have heard all the speakers once.
- Note your answers and then use the second listening to check them.

Part 4

Part 4 is usually a conversation, about three minutes in length. There are seven questions. These may be 'choose the best answer **A**, **B** or **C**' or some other type, such as True/False. You only have to write a letter for each answer. There is time to read the questions through before you listen to the conversation, a short pause after you hear it, and then it is repeated.

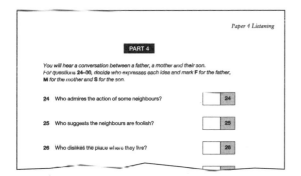

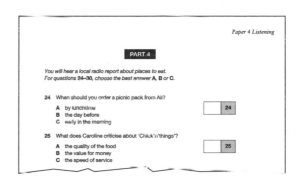

- The questions usually contain lots of helpful information about how the conversation develops, so read them carefully to get an idea of what you're going to hear.
- Be careful not to choose your answers too quickly. Speakers may appear to be saying one thing at the beginning of a speech and then change direction (e.g. *I'd like to come out this evening … but I've got too much homework.*)
- Sentences with linking words (like *but, although, if*) can cause you problems because speakers don't usually emphasise these words. If you miss the linking word, you may get the wrong idea, so make sure you know all the common linking words and can recognise them easily. Be especially careful with words which sound similar, such as *so/though, why/while, also/although*.

Paper 5 Speaking

About the Speaking paper

The Speaking paper is your chance to show how well you can use spoken English to give and exchange information and opinions. You will be examined with a partner, as this allows the examiners to test more skills than they could in a one-to-one conversation with you. There are two examiners: an *interlocutor*, who explains the tasks and asks the questions, and an *assessor*, who does not take part in the conversation, but concentrates on giving marks for what you say.

The Speaking paper lasts approximately fifteen minutes and is divided into four parts. You need to use your English in different ways, from simply talking about yourself at the start to working on particular tasks in the later parts of the paper, when you have to discuss problems with your partner and try to reach agreement.

- You will get good marks if you:
  - work well with your partner to carry out the tasks correctly
  - speak with clear pronunciation
  - speak with reasonably natural speed and rhythm
  - use a variety of grammar
  - use a variety of appropriate vocabulary.

- When you look at a list like this, it is important to remember that First Certificate is an intermediate examination. The examiners do not expect you to sound exactly like someone whose first language is English, or to have perfect grammar. You should always think about what you are saying, but don't let the fear of making mistakes prevent you from speaking freely.

Study notes

The timings below are for all the work in each part of the paper. Part 1, for instance, includes your turn, your partner's turn and the examiner's instructions to both of you. You personally will probably not speak for much more than one minute out of the four minutes allowed for this part.

Part 1

Part 1 (about four minutes) gives you the chance to get used to your partner and the examiners while you talk about familiar topics like your personal background, interests, etc. Each student has a separate turn. This part of the paper tests mainly social language.

- Be ready to talk in this part, even if you are naturally a quiet person. If the examiner asks you what you do in your free time, for instance, don't just say that you 'go out with friends'. If you do, you may not make any mistakes, but you will not show the examiner much about your English, either. *Where do you go? What do you do? Why do you enjoy it?* Talking about any of these will make you use different grammar and more vocabulary. Remember that the idea of the paper is to show what you can do, not to hide your English away so no one can criticise.

Part 2

In Part 2 (about four minutes), the examiner will give you two colour photos and ask you to talk about the photos and ideas connected with them. You can talk generally or about your own experience of the topic, if you have any. Your partner will also have a pair of pictures to talk about. This part of the paper tests your ability to give information and to express opinions.

- It will normally be useful to mention what the pictures show, but don't fall into the trap of just listing all the details you can see in the picture. If you do this, there is a chance that what you actually say will be very simple and that you will use the same grammar over and over again (*There is …; There are …; I can see …*). You wouldn't do this in your own language, and, if you prepare wisely for the examination, there is no reason for you to do it in English.

- When you first see the pictures, think why the examiners have put them together. For example, a picture of a man in a garden reading a book, together with a photo of a woman water-skiing might show two different ways of relaxing: *Which do you think is better?* or *Do you like both for different reasons?* etc. Points like these develop the conversation in a natural way and will give you a good idea of what questions the examiner might ask you. It's probably not very important in this case whether the man is wearing glasses or not and, if you talk about such small details, you may never even reach the main point of the two photos. You will also have no idea what the examiner will ask you afterwards.

- Listen carefully to everything your partner says in Parts 1 and 2. There may be an opportunity to ask a question or comment on what they say, but more importantly, you need to get used to how they speak (speed, accent, type of vocabulary, etc.) before you start working with them in Part 3. Even if you already know the person, they may be nervous or be 'putting on a show' and this may change the way they speak. You can judge whether, in Parts 3 and 4, you might need to interrupt them politely (if they are excited and can't stop talking) or ask them to repeat something (if they speak quietly or you don't understand). Turn situations like these to your advantage by learning and using appropriate expressions: for example, *I'm sorry, could you say that again?* makes a much better impression on the examiners than *What?* or *What did you say?*

Part 3

In Part 3 (about three minutes), you and your partner work together. The examiner will give you both something to look at (map, advertisements, photographs, etc.), and ask you to work together to make a plan, take a decision, solve a problem, etc. While you and your partner are working on the task, the examiner will not say much, but will help you if you have problems. This part of the paper tests your ability to use your English to co-operate with other people on a task. This involves exchanging information and opinions, taking turns and directing the conversation when necessary.

- Make sure you and your partner understand the task before you begin. Don't be afraid to ask the examiner if you are not sure what to do. This can happen just as easily in 'real life', and the ability to deal politely and successfully with difficulties like this can show that you really know how to use your English.

Part 4

In Part 4 (about four minutes), the examiner will ask you both to discuss ideas connected with the work you did in Part 3, and will ask you both questions to give you the chance to cover the topic fully. This part of the paper tests the ability to express opinions and comment appropriately on other people's views. Taking turns and co-operation with your partner can be important here, too.

- The examiner will ask questions to develop ideas from Part 3, but doesn't want to hear you saying the same things over again. Listen carefully to the questions and try to take the discussion into areas which you haven't already discussed.
- In Parts 3 and 4, try to share the time equally with your partner. Ideally, the conversation should pass quite freely between you. If your partner is quiet, you may need to ask direct questions (e.g. *What do you think about…? Do you think that's a good idea?* etc.). If your partner talks a bit too much, you must be prepared to interrupt politely and give your own opinion (e.g. *Yes, I see what you mean, but …*). When you are practising, try to find out whether you are too quiet or talk too much yourself (your friends may help you to decide!). Like any 'real-life' conversation, the exercises work best when the two speakers are aware of each other's needs. There are many good books on spoken English which can help you to learn how to 'manage' a conversation successfully.

Preparing for the examination

- Try to get as much practical speaking experience as you can. You will be with a partner in the Speaking paper, so practise with a partner whenever you can. This may be difficult, or impossible, in your particular situation, but it is difficult to be relaxed about the exercises, or to understand completely how they work, if you haven't had some practice. Ask a friend or relative to help. Even if their English isn't as good as yours, you will get some experience of managing the exercises and the timing – and you'll probably have a good laugh, too.
- You can also play all three parts yourself (examiner and both students). This is not as stupid as it sounds – although you may still want to make sure that no one else can hear you! The main disadvantages are that you don't get any listening practice, and, as you will be in complete control of the situation, you will not have to deal with any unexpected difficulties. If you work like this, don't let your voice go flat. Like a radio announcer, or an actor talking into a telephone on stage, you have to imagine that people are really listening to you.
- Do not spend too long looking at the practice pictures in this book before you actually use them because, in the examination, you will not see the pictures in advance, and will have to think quickly and start talking almost immediately. This is an important skill to practise: you must get used to starting quickly, even if this means you have to start talking before you know exactly what you want to say. You do this all the time in your own language, often by using 'fillers' – phrases which do not mean much in themselves, but give you time to think while you are talking. You can learn to do this in English, too, with phrases like *I'm not sure what the best answer is, but perhaps …*; *I haven't really thought about this before, but I suppose …*, etc. If you have to learn new phrases to do this, make sure you do it early, and get lots of practice with the ones you like. Also, make sure you don't emphasise fillers too strongly. You can probably hear how strange this sounds if you do it in your own language: fillers don't add much to the meaning of what you say, so they don't need strong emphasis.

- **Remember:** the Speaking paper is an opportunity to show your ability, not a threat. The examiners choose the exercises as good starting points for conversation, not to cause you problems on particular points of vocabulary or grammar. However, it is a good idea to make sure that you have enough general vocabulary to be able to talk about any of the 25 topic areas listed on page 28. If nothing else, this will make you feel more confident when you go into the examination room.

- Notice that much of what you have to say in the examination room is **not** directly concerned with the topics of Parts 2, 3 and 4. If you study and practise the language you need in order to introduce yourself, meet new people, express opinions, make suggestions, take turns, disagree politely, apologise for mistakes, etc., you will soon be on the way to a good mark. Skills like these are what the test is really about, not the photographs and diagrams which are used in the various exercises.

- It is also useful to do some work on explaining where something is in a picture or diagram (*the man in the background, the house in the top left-hand corner*) or how it relates to other things in the picture (*the tallest woman, the house opposite the cinema*). Try to avoid pointing things out with your finger.

- Get into the habit of talking about the other work you are doing – texts you have read, films you have seen, articles you have produced for the Writing paper, etc. If you can find someone to listen to you, so much the better, but this is not essential. Too many students learn languages in their heads without getting the words out of their mouths often enough to become really confident. Don't be one of them.

Practice

Practice 1

Part 1

Ask each other about the area where you live. Use questions like these:

Where are you from?
What part of ... are you from?
How long have you lived in ... ?
Tell me a bit about the area ...
What's it like living here/there ... ?
(if you are not in your home town/country) *What are the main differences between here and your home town/country?*

Each of you should try to talk naturally about these things for about two minutes.

Part 2

One of you looks at pictures 1A and 1B in the Colour Section. Show the pictures to your partner. Talk about your pictures for one minute while your partner listens. Say what your pair of pictures shows. Mention ways in which they are similar and different. Say how you feel about them. Talk for about one minute. Ask your partner which of them she (or he) prefers. Now, the person who has been listening talks about pictures 1C and 1D in the same way and then asks the listener which of them she (or he) prefers.

Part 3

Look at the plan of a youth centre (1E) together. Decide how you would use the different rooms. For example, think about where the café should be, or the toilets. Spend about two or three minutes discussing this.

Part 4

Now imagine the examiner joins your conversation and asks you questions. Practise answering questions about what you have been discussing. For example, you can ask each other questions like these:

> *Have you ever been to a youth centre?/Did you use a youth centre when you were a teenager?*
> *Do you think it is important to have places where young people can meet? Why or why not?*
> *What kinds of activities should youth centres offer?*
> *How often should they be open and at what times of day?*
> *How should they be paid for?*
> *Do you think there are enough places for young people to go in their free time?*
> *Are young people offered too much entertainment nowadays? Does this mean they aren't used to amusing themselves?*
> *Do you think some crimes happen because young people haven't got enough to do? What can be done about this?*

This part of the test lasts about four minutes.

Practice 2

Part 1

Ask each other about your families. Use questions like these:

> *Do you have brothers and sisters? Tell me something about them ...*
> *Do you get on well together?*
> *What are the advantages/disadvantages of being an only child/member of a large family?*
> *Do you see much of the older members of your family? Your grandparents, for example?*

Each of you should try to talk naturally about these things for about two minutes.

Part 2

One of you looks at pictures 2A and 2B in the Colour Section. Show the pictures to your partner. Talk about your pictures for one minute while your partner listens. Say what your pair of pictures shows. Mention ways in which they are similar and different. Say how you'd feel about looking for clothes in similar places. Talk for about one minute. Ask your partner which of them she (or he) would prefer to buy clothes in. Now, the person who has been listening talks about pictures 2C and 2D in the same way and then asks the listener which of them she (or he) would prefer to buy clothes in.

Part 3

Look at the pictures in 2E together. They show items you might want to have in a study bedroom. Discuss which of the items each of you would choose to have in your rooms and tell each other why.

Spend about two or three minutes doing this.

Part 4

Now imagine the examiner joins your conversation and asks you questions. Practise answering questions related to what you have been discussing. For example, you can ask each other questions like these:

Are there any other things you would want in a room of your own?

Are your possessions important to you? What kinds of things are most important?

Do you think it is important for people to have a room of their own to study in?

Are you a tidy person? How important is it to you to keep a room tidy?

Have you ever shared a room or an office with anyone? How did you get on? Were there any problems?

This part of the test lasts about four minutes.

Practice 3

Part 1

Ask each other about free-time activities. Use questions like these:

What do you enjoy doing in your free time?

Tell me a bit about what you actually do when you …

How long have you been interested in … ?

Can you explain something about the rules of / why people enjoy / the attraction of … ?

Each of you should try to talk naturally about these things for about two minutes.

Part 2

One of you looks at pictures 3A and 3B in the Colour Section. Show the pictures to your partner. Talk about your pictures for one minute while your partner listens. Say what your pair of pictures shows. Mention ways in which they are similar and different. Say whether you think these sports are enjoyable or not. Talk for about one minute. Ask your partner which sport she (or he) thinks would be most enjoyable. Now, the person who has been listening talks about pictures 3C and 3D in the same way and then asks the listener which sport she (or he) thinks would be most enjoyable.

Part 3

Look at the illustrations (3E) which show different ways of improving or protecting the environment. Discuss which of them is most helpful for the environment. Discuss the costs as well.

Spend about two or three minutes doing this.

Part 4

Now imagine the examiner joins your conversation and asks you questions. Practise answering questions related to what you have been discussing. For example, you can ask each other questions like these:

> *Do you think enough money is spent on the environment?*
> *If you had some money to spend on an environmental project, how would you spend it?*
> *Are most people in your country interested in protecting the environment? Do you think they should be more aware?*
> *How can people be educated to care about the environment?*
> *Are there other problems which are more important than the environment that we should spend time and money on?*

This part of the test lasts about four minutes.

Practice 4

Part 1

Ask each other about studying English. Use questions like these:

> *Are you studying English for any special purpose?*
> *In what way do you think English will be useful to you in the future? If not, why not?*
> *What other languages do you/would you like to study? Why?*
> *Can you tell me about your career plans?*
> (If you are still at school) *What will you do when you leave school?*

Each of you should try to talk naturally about these things for about two minutes.

Part 2

One of you looks at pictures 4A and 4B in the Colour Section. Show the pictures to your partner. Talk about your pictures for one minute while your partner listens. Say what your pair of pictures shows. Mention ways in which they are similar and different. Say whether you'd like to listen to these types of music or not. Talk for about one minute. Ask your partner which of them she (or he) would prefer to listen to. Now, the person who has been listening talks about pictures 4C and 4D in the same way and then asks the listener which of them she (or he) would prefer to listen to.

Part 3

Look at the illustrations in 4E together. They show different ways of campaigning to prevent a swimming-pool from being closed down. You want the pool to stay open. Discuss which of these ways of campaigning is likely to be most successful.

Spend about two or three minutes doing this.

Part 4

Now imagine the examiner joins your conversation and asks you questions. Practise answering questions related to what you have been discussing. For example, you can ask each other questions like these:

> *Have you ever tried to stop something happening? What did you do?*

Do you think people have enough control over what happens in the area they live in? Who makes decisions about this sort of thing?
Is enough money spent on facilities like swimming-pools in your town?
What sort of places for sport or entertainment would you like to see opened around where you live?

This part of the test lasts for about four minutes.

FCE topics

These are the topics used in the FCE exam:
- Personal life and circumstances e.g. personal experiences
- Living conditions e.g. where/how people live
- Occupations
- Education, study and learning
- Free-time activities
- Travel and tourism
- Consumer goods and shopping
- Eating and drinking
- Social/family relations
- The media
- The weather
- The environment/ecology
- Entertainment
- Health and exercise
- Services e.g. banks, post offices, etc.
- Places
- Language
- Music
- Fashion
- Animals
- Cinema
- History
- The Arts
- Sports
- People

Taking the exam

Some time before the examination takes place, you will be told the dates and times of your papers, and where the examination will be held. Make a careful note of your Centre number and particularly your Candidate number.

Papers 1, 2 and **3** always take place on the same day. **Papers 4** and **5** will probably take place on one or two different days close to the written papers. At some centres, all five papers take place on the same day. Whichever is the case at your centre, make sure you understand and follow the instructions carefully and arrive in good time. If the building where the examination is held is new to you, it is a good idea to allow enough time to deal with problems (not being able to find the right entrance, going to the wrong room, etc.), so that you can arrive at your desk calm and ready to start work. This is especially important if you think you may be nervous on the examination day.

Before you start

Check all the examination materials you are given (question papers, answer sheets, marksheet, etc.) to make sure that they are the correct level, i.e. First Certificate, and if they come with a candidate name already printed on, that the material carries your own name. If anything seems to be wrong, tell the supervisor immediately. Do not wait until the end of the examination, when it may be too late to do anything about it.

This is also important in the Listening paper. If you cannot hear the tape properly during the introduction to the examination, you must tell the supervisor immediately. Nothing can be done if you complain after the test.

If for any reason, in any paper, you have to write answers on extra sheets of paper, be sure to write your name, Centre number and Candidate number clearly at the top of each extra sheet. Do this before you begin each sheet: it is too easy to forget at the end. Make sure that any extra sheets are safely attached to the rest of your work.

Writing your answers

For **Papers 1, 3** and **4** you will be provided with special answer sheets. You should study the samples at the back of this book carefully and make sure that you understand how to use them. If you can, make photocopies and practise answering on the answer sheets at an early stage, so that you can get used to dealing with them. You do not want to have difficulty with the sheets in the examination itself. In **Paper 2,** you answer in the question paper booklet (e.g. Test 1 pages 45 and 47).

Many candidates prefer to mark their answers on the question paper first, and then copy them onto the answer sheet later. If you prefer to do this, you must learn to answer the questions quickly enough to allow plenty of time to put your answers on the answer sheet before the end of the paper **without**

rushing. If you have to hurry, you may make mistakes by copying your answers wrongly, or by putting your answers against the wrong question numbers.

Paper 1

1	A B C D E F G H I
2	A B C D E F G H I
3	A B C D E F G H I

For Paper 1 you need a soft pencil and a good quality eraser. Notice that the answer sheet includes nine choices (**A–I**) for each question number, although the question paper itself will have fewer choices for many of the questions (e.g. four choices in Part 2). Just ignore the unnecessary letters. The diagram above shows the answers marked in for Questions 1 and 2 of an imaginary Paper 1. The answer for Question 1 is E and the answer for Question 2 is G. These marks **must** be made in **pencil.** If you change your mind, **you must rub out your first answer completely** since two marks against any question number will automatically be marked wrong. Be sure to work cleanly on the answer sheet. This answer sheet will be 'read' by an electronic 'eye' and any dirty marks may be misinterpreted by it.

Part 4 of Paper 1 may include questions which require more than one correct answer. For example, a task based on four short texts about different museums might ask:

Which museum:
has recently opened a new building?

22		23	

In this case, you may give the two answers you choose in any order.

This only happens in Part 4 of Paper 1, and you will find that such answers are marked 'interchangeable' in the Key.

- Practise filling in the answer sheet **while you are answering the questions** on Paper 1; don't wait to copy your answers at the end. (Remember, you are allowed to photocopy the answer sheets at the end of this book, so you can have plenty of practice with them.)
- Always make sure you are putting your answer against the correct question number. This is especially important when you leave out a difficult question and move on.
- There are two reasons why it's better to write straight onto the answer sheet. First, you **save time,** which can be important on Paper 1. Second, you **avoid mistakes in** copying.

Paper 2

You must write your answers for Paper 2 in the spaces provided on the question paper. You **must** write in **pen** and you must hand in all your rough notes and plans at the end of the test. If you want to change something, cross it out neatly.

Don't use brackets ( ) for this. Write as clearly as possible. This paper is marked by examiners and tidy, legible work is much appreciated. Bad handwriting or messy changes to your answer can actually lose marks if your final decisions are not clear.

- Remember how important it is to plan your answer before you begin. This should mean that you do not need to change to a new question or rewrite large parts of your answer on the examination paper.

Papers 3 and 4

Paper 3:

Part 1						Part 2		Do not write here
1	A	B	C	D		16		☐ 16 ☐
2	A	B	C	D		17		☐ 17 ☐
3	A	B	C	D		18		18

Paper 4:

Part 1				Part 2		Do not write here
1	A	B	C	9		☐ 9 ☐
2	A	B	C	10		☐ 10 ☐
3	A	B	C	11		11

For these papers, it is quite a good idea to **write your answers on the question paper** and then **transfer** them to the special answer sheet. There is usually plenty of time during Paper 3 to do this and for Paper 4 you are given five minutes at the end of the test.

Both papers involve two different answering methods.

Paper 3, Part 1
Paper 4, Parts 1 and 3
These are like smaller versions of Paper 1. You must answer **in pencil**, and take special care when making any changes (as described for Paper 1 on page 30).

Paper 3, Parts 2, 3, 4 and 5
Paper 4, Parts 2 and 4
In these parts, you must write your answers in the spaces provided. It's best to write **in pen**, although you can use pencil if you wish. Be careful not to make spelling mistakes when you are copying and do not make any marks in the columns headed 'Do not write here'. These are used for marking your answers.

- With the Listening paper, as with the Speaking (see below), it is a good idea to spend the time immediately before your test getting yourself ready to work in English. Find someone to talk to in English, or concentrate quietly on the task ahead. Avoid friends who want to chat in your own language – you will have plenty of time for that afterwards!

Paper 5

It's worth remembering some general advice when you think about the Speaking paper: find out exactly where it is and get there in good time, but not too early if you think this will make you nervous. The supervisor will give you a computerised marksheet to hand to the examiner at the start of your test. This looks similar to the written answer sheets at the back of this book. Make sure it has your name on it – you don't want someone else to get your mark!

You will then go into the exam room with your partner, the examiners will ask you for your marksheet and check that it has the correct name. Then the test begins. Remember that one of the examiners will not be joining in the conversation, and may sit some distance away in a corner. You should concentrate on the examiner working with you (the interlocutor) and on your partner. Do not worry about the other examiner during the test.

At the end of the test, the examiner will thank you both. You should thank the examiners and leave promptly. The examiners will keep your marksheet, and they are not allowed to discuss your marks with you, so do not ask them how you have done.

- You may have a chance to say hello to your exam partner before the test begins. If you do, do not miss this opportunity to get to know each other.
- You will get off to a better start if you have been speaking and/or thinking in English before the examination. This will help you to have your vocabulary close to the front of your mind, and to have your best pronunciation ready. Candidates often make the mistake of spending the last half hour before their test chatting to friends in their own language. Unless you are very good indeed, this is not the best preparation for a test in a foreign language!
- It is also a good idea to go through in your mind what you will have to do in the different parts of the Paper, so that you are ready to do the right job at the right time.
- If you get very nervous, it can be helpful to do some deep-breathing exercises before you go in. Remind yourself that you have done a lot of work for this, and that this is your chance to show it.

Results

When you receive your result, you will be given a **grade** for the whole exam. If you get A (the highest grade), B or C, you have passed, and will receive a **certificate.** If you get D, E or U (Unclassified), you have failed, and will not receive a certificate.

All candidates receive a **results slip.** If you pass the exam, your results slip will mention any papers in which you did particularly well. For example, it might show that your exam grade is C, but you scored particularly good marks in the Speaking paper. If you fail the exam, your results slip will show you the papers in which you did badly. This will help if you decide to try again, because you will know where you need the most practice.

The Practice Tests

Practice Test 1

PART 1

You are going to read a magazine article about air pollution. Choose from the list (**A–H**) *the sentence which best summarises each part* (**1–6**) *of the article. There is an extra sentence which you do not need to use. There is an example at the beginning* (**0**).
Mark your answers **on the separate answer sheet**.

A	Research is being done into electric cars.
B	People refuse to give up their cars in cities.
C	One answer is to persuade people to buy electric cars.
D	Cities where people depend heavily on cars have the worst problems.
E	Electric cars have a major disadvantage.
F	Air pollution appears to be a cause of illness.
G	Air pollution is now a worry for everyone.
H	Cars are destroying the air quality in cities.

Cars switch on to plugged-in power

0	*H*

Around the world, governments and their citizens are becoming increasingly concerned about what the motor car and its internal combustion engine do to the air we breathe. In some cities, air pollution resulting from the internal combustion engine is so bad that drastic action has had to be taken. In summertime, pollution in some southern European cities is now so serious that it is common for half the usual number of commuters to be forbidden to bring their cars into the city.

1	*7*

Calculating the number of people who become unwell or even die as a result of air pollution is very difficult. But recent studies of the effects of car fumes suggest that the health risks may be more severe than previously thought.

2	*G*

Suddenly, urban air pollution is no longer a subject just for environmentalists but a cause of widespread public concern. Ordinary people are beginning to sit up and take notice.

3	*A C*

There are numerous proposed ways of dealing with the problem: one of the most radical is to slowly stop using the internal combustion engine and to use instead the electric motor powered from a large battery pack. A lot of money is now being invested by car and battery manufacturers to create 'clean' vehicles.

4	*D*

Much of the pressure has come from the land where the car is king – California. The United States has no public transport to speak of (the major car-makers actively contributed to its destruction) so the car is the average American's only practical means of daily transport. But some US cities, Los Angeles in particular, are paying a high price for this over-reliance. LA's famous smogs – trapped by the natural 'bowl' of the nearby mountains – are the result of reactions between the chemicals which come from the city's millions of car exhausts.

5	*D A*

Because of this serious pollution problem, California has for over 20 years set tough pollution laws. Even so, LA's smog problem has not been solved. So now, the 'sunshine state' has taken the first step towards removing the internal combustion engine altogether from its roads. From 1998, all car-makers who sell their cars in California will have to offer a proportion of electric cars for sale. In 1998 the proportion of electric cars offered must be two per cent, rising to five per cent by 2003 and to ten per cent by 2005.

6	*A*

Environmentalists argue, with some justification, that only by making laws like this can politicians force change on the car industry. But others – some of them no less committed to cleaner urban air – doubt that the totally electric car is the right solution to the problem. The difficulty with electric cars is that they can only travel a short distance at a time. At the moment there is no obvious solution to the transport problems of the world's cities.

PART 2

You are going to read a newspaper article about backpacking. For questions
7–14, *choose the answer* (**A, B, C** *or* **D**) *which you think fits best according to the*
text.
Mark your answers **on the separate answer sheet**.

Self-made satisfaction

IT HAD been a long, hard, wonderful day.
The two of us had walked from the sea's edge
through the length of a beautiful valley,
climbed a superb mountain, traversed its
5 narrow, rocky ridge, and now stood on its
final peak, tired, happy and looking for the
perfect camp site.

The experienced backpacker has a natural
feeling for such things, and our eyes were
10 drawn to a small blue circle on the map, like
an eye winking at us. We could not see it from
where we were, but we followed our
judgement and descended steeply until it came
into view.

We were right. It was a calm pool, with flat 15
grass beside it. Gently taking our packs off,
we made the first of many cups of tea before
putting up our tent. Later that evening, over
another cup of tea and after a good meal, we
sat outside the tent watching the sun set over a 20
glittering sea dotted with islands, towards one
of which a ferry was slowly moving. It is not
always so perfect, of course. On another trip,
with a different companion, a thoroughly wet
day had ended at a lonely farm. Depressed at 25
the thought of camping, we had knocked and
asked if we could use a barn as a shelter.

Backpacking could be defined as the art of

comfortable, self-sufficient travel on foot. Everything you need is in the pack on your back, and you become emotionally as well as physically attached to it. I once left my pack hidden in some rocks while I made a long trip to a peak I particularly wanted to climb. I was away for nearly three hours and ended up running the last stretch in fear that my precious pack would not be there. It was, of course.

The speed at which the backpacker travels makes this the perfect way to see any country. You experience the landscape as a slow unfolding scene, almost in the way it was made; and you find time to stop and talk to people you meet. I've learned much local history from simply chatting to people met while walking through an area. At the end of a trip, whether three days or three weeks, there's a good feeling of achievement, of having got somewhere under your own power.

After years of going out walking just for the day, many people start backpacking simply through wanting to stay out rather than cut short a trip.

In Britain, the backpacker is necessarily restricted and directed to a degree. There are no areas completely untouched by humans, though we do have fine wild country. In the north-west of Scotland, I have managed to walk for three days without crossing a road or passing an inhabited house. In the lowlands, your overnight stops may have to be on recognised camp sites. In upland country, you have the priceless gift of choosing where to camp. Even here, many factors come into play, and I shan't easily forget a night camped on a ski run surrounded by fences: we were simply too tired to go any further.

There is one important rule the good backpacker should follow: respect the land and its people – as the Americans say, 'take only photographs (one might add memories), leave only footprints'.

With good equipment, you can survive just about anything the weather can throw at you – and modern equipment is very good indeed. Of course, you need to know how to use it – go to a specialist outdoor shop for good advice. In particular, you need to be confident in map reading.

As with any other sport, start gently and locally, improve your skills and gradually widen your horizons. Britain is only crowded in patches and there is still plenty of space for the backpacker wanting to be alone.

7   The writer and his companion knew there was a pool because
   A   they had seen it earlier in the day.
   B   they had been told about it.
   C   they could see it on the map.
   D   they could see it from the top of the mountain.

8   What does 'it' refer to in line 13?
   A   the pool
   B   the mountain
   C   the camp site
   D   the map

9   How did they feel at the end of the day?
   A   They wished they could have found a farm.
   B   They were delighted with the spot they'd found.
   C   They were anxious about the weather to come.
   D   They were too tired to put up their tent.

10 What does the writer mean by being 'emotionally as well as physically attached' to his backpack (lines 31–32)?
   A He might die on the mountains without it.
   B It is not a good idea to leave it anywhere.
   C He walks better when he is wearing it.
   D It is more than just a practical aid.

11 According to the writer, the main advantage of backpacking is that you can
   A find out how the landscape was made.
   B gain an understanding of the area you walk through.
   C make new friends while walking.
   D get fitter as you walk.

12 What does the writer mean by 'the priceless gift of choosing where to camp' (lines 63–64)?
   A It is not usually possible to camp wherever you want.
   B Camp sites are often quite expensive.
   C Some of the camp sites are difficult to reach.
   D Some areas do not have suitable camp sites for backpackers.

13 What advice does the writer give about backpacking?
   A You should take lots of photographs to remind you of your trip.
   B You should avoid spending too much on equipment.
   C You should first walk in an area you are familiar with.
   D You should only go out in suitable weather.

14 What difference between backpacking and walking does the writer mention?
   A Backpackers travel in pairs or groups.
   B Backpackers never sleep indoors.
   C Backpackers' routes are carefully planned.
   D Backpackers' walks last longer than a day.

PART 3

*You are going to read a magazine article about a violinist. Seven paragraphs have been removed from the article. Choose from the paragraphs (**A–H**) the one which fits each gap (**15–20**). There is one extra paragraph which you do not need to use. There is an example at the beginning (**0**).*

*Mark your answers **on the separate answer sheet**.*

Where's the Festival Hall?

'Where's the Festival Hall from here?' The question leaves me a little surprised. Joshua Bell and I are gazing out from his room in London's Savoy Hotel – straight at the Festival Hall, in fact. Cautiously, I point out the building, but little surprise registers on his much photographed face. Perhaps it's the jet lag.

0   *H*

'Actually, I think I manage touring better than many,' he declares. 'It doesn't really bother me, because I happen to like going to new places and I love hotels. I don't even mind long transatlantic flights. At this point it's still exciting for me.' He does need to escape every so often though, and I had already found this out.

15   *A̶ B*

He apologises: 'I'd been on the road and realised I had four complete full days off. I think I was in Scotland and had to be in Cologne five days later. I felt like I just needed to get home, so I hopped on a plane.'

16   *C*

'My teacher, Josef Gingold, encouraged me to perform as much as I could, to get out there and do it. I think the fact that I was so young then and on stage might be one of the reasons why I feel comfortable on stage now. I don't feel like it's something foreign. I feel that's where I can do my best work, and so I don't get anxious or anything like that.'

17   *E*

'It was the first time I'd played with a major orchestra, and I clearly remember the feeling of hearing such a polished sound; I was just blown away by it.'

18   *D*

Three years after that, Bell made his first tour to Europe with the St Louis Symphony Orchestra, and his first London performance happened the following year. And it was around then, too, that he began to make a lot of appearances in

the advertising pages of the music press.

19   *G*

Did he think such publicity was damaging? 'Well, not in the long run. In the end, people will judge me for what I do, and if they don't like me for that, that's fine. I would hate for someone to judge me just on what they think of record companies. I heard of several critics who said they wouldn't even listen to my records.'

20   *A*

Bell has indeed outlived that image. His playing has consistently drawn praise for its effortless mastery and beautiful tone.

A After nine years of doing concert tours, Bell knows when he needs a break. He feels the early start to his career was very useful.

B What did he think of that? 'It was unfortunate, but it's been several years since then. And people in the music world did get to know who I was in a fairly short time. But it's only now that I've stopped hearing about it, even in the good reviews.'

C Bell also remembers the warmth shown him by the members of the orchestra: 'At that time I was the youngest ever to have played in a subscription concert there. They heard I collected coins and several of the players gave me things from their own collections. It was a nice feeling.'

D This is my second attempt at meeting the fresh-faced American violinist: I remind him that, a few weeks earlier, the first attempt failed because of his sudden decision to fly home to New York.

E 'It's unfortunate that most instrumentalists today don't write their own music. In the old days everybody did. I've no idea if I'd be successful at writing music, but it's something I'd love to do.'

F He now admits to feeling uncomfortable about the boy-next-door image his record company seemed eager to present at that time, especially in the light of the reaction it caused in Britain, where he was not as well-known as he was back home in the States.

G There were no nerves, according to Bell, when at 14 he did his first professional concerto performance with the Philadelphia Orchestra. Naturally, though, the occasion made a lasting impression.

H Throughout our interview, Bell yawns and rubs his eyes. I begin to feel bad about not letting him sleep.

PART 4

You are going to read a magazine article about women writers. For questions
21–35, *choose from the people* (**A–E**). *Some of the people may be chosen more
than once. When more than one answer is required, these may be given in any
order. There is an example at the beginning* (**0**).
Mark your answers **on the separate answer sheet**.

A	Gill Coleridge
B	Margaret Drabble
C	Margaret Forster
D	Frances Fyfield
E	Ruth Rendell

Which woman makes the following statement?

Male and female authors do not write in the same way.	**0**	*B*		
Women's attitudes to life are reflected in today's fiction.	**21**	*C*		
Men could profit from reading novels written by women.	**22**	*E*		
She does not aim her writing at men or women in particular.	**23**	*A*	**24**	*B*
Authors write about things they feel comfortable with.	**25**	*A B* ✓		
You can't always guess whether a book is by a man or a woman.	**26**	*B*		
Fiction written for men tends to have a strong storyline.	**27**	*D*		
An equal number of men and women react to her books.	**28**	*B C* ✓		
Some women have been her fans for a long time.	**29**	*B C*		

She aims her writing mainly at women.

| 30 | |

She doesn't change her writing because of what other people might think.

| 31 | |

Women readers like to get emotionally involved with the characters in a novel.

| 32 | B |

Her main aim is for her books to be interesting.

| 33 | |

Authors who want financial success aim at a particular type of reader.

| 34 | |

Women like reading about other women who lead more fulfilled lives.

| 35 | |

Is what we believe about women writers fact or fiction?

Women read more than men: that's official. And statistically, what do they like reading best? Novels. Novels about love, novels about crime, novels that are funny, clever and deep but above all, novels written by other women.

There is, of course, an enormous difference between 'popular' and 'literary' fiction. As literary agent **Gill Coleridge** explains, 'In the commercial side of the business, the most important feature of male fiction is the plot, whereas in female fiction it is characters that the reader can identify with and care about. Commercial authors focus on a chosen audience, writers of literary novels write what they want to say.'

Margaret Drabble, who has written several successful literary novels, says that she never imagines her reader to be male or female when she sits down to write. 'That person changes from chapter to chapter. Sometimes I think about friends – I bet Judith would like this or James would hate that, but it doesn't affect what I write. There's been a change in the last two or three decades in how a whole generation of women look at the world and therefore what they accept in their fiction. Luckily for me, a fairly loyal readership of women has grown old along with me, taken the same journey. But because men and women react differently to things, there is a difference in how male and female authors write. We tend to write about things we like and which are sympathetic to us.' She claims to be much more aware now of the male reader, because the different worlds which men and women live in are less separate nowadays than they used to be.

As a novelist and biographer (she has written the life stories of several well-known people), **Margaret Forster** says of the letters she receives from readers that men and women write to her in equal numbers. Of women readers she says, 'Women are hungry for details of other people's lives, particularly women's lives: biography as well as fiction provides that second-hand experience. Many women get to middle age and wonder where their life has gone, why they haven't made more of it: reading about others who have achieved something enlarges their vision.'

Crime writer **Frances Fyfield** wishes that more men would read more fiction, especially by women. 'If all you read is thrillers and adventures, you're bound to have a gap of knowledge. I write very much with the female reader in mind, though I take my male readers into account too.'

Crime writer **Ruth Rendell** says she cannot always tell male writing from female writing: 'Women are always credited with being better at writing detail, men with taking the wider view. But I've just been rereading Anthony Powell's *A Dance To The Music Of Time* and it's full of detail. Just as many men as women read my books. I don't think of my audience as being one or the other, only that there shouldn't be too many things that they find dull.'

PAPER 2 WRITING (1 hour 30 minutes)

*You **must** answer this question.*

1   You have received a letter from a friend, asking for information about a
    swimming course you attended last year.

> By the way, my brother is thinking of taking his family on
> a swimming course this summer. He and his wife are serious
> swimmers, but their children are very young and can't swim yet
> so they're looking for somewhere with plenty of variety. Did
> you have a good time when you went to Merle Park? I seem to
> remember you had a few problems.
>   Could you let me know what you thought of the place, and
> whether you think they would enjoy it? Thanks.
>
> Best wishes
>
> *Stephen*

Read the letter carefully, and look at the leaflet from last year's courses, on
which you have written some notes. Then write to your friend, answering his
questions and explaining whether this course would be suitable or not.

Merle Park Aquacentre

* 7-day Swimming courses for all ages and abilities
* Pools open 6.00 am daily
* Full-sized pool
* Weight-training room
* Ex-national coach — *very strict*
* Separate learner and fun pools
* Wave machine
* Sporting Sam Club – games and competitions for children
* Full programme of evening entertainment — *noisy!*
* Excursions to local beauty spots — *too tired*

Write a **letter** of between **120–180** words in an appropriate style on the next
page. Do not write any addresses.

PART 1

PART 2

*Write an answer to **one** of the questions **2–5** in this part. Write your answer in **120–180** words in an appropriate style on the next page, putting the question number in the box.*

2

> # —— **Sunrise Travel** ——
> ## announce their
> # *Summer Fun Competition.*
>
> Three lucky winners will receive two weeks' holiday, all expenses paid, at a destination of their choice.
>
> To take part, all you have to do is describe the best or worst holiday you have ever had.

Write your **description** for the travel company's competition.

3   A student magazine has asked readers to send in short stories which include the sentence: **All at once I began to understand why I was being treated so well**.

Write your **story**.

4   Your local tourist information office is putting together a leaflet for visitors. You have been asked to write a report on shopping facilities in your area.

Write your **report**.

5   **Background reading texts**

Answer **one** of the following two questions based on your reading of **one** of the set books (see p. 2). Write the title of the book next to the question number box.

Either   **(a)**   Describe the events which lead up to the most important moment in the story.

or   **(b)**   Describe some of the most important people in the book and explain how they affect the story.

PART 2

Question	

....

....

....

....

....

....

....

....

....

....

....

....

....

....

....

....

....

....

....

....

....

....

....

....

....

....

....

PAPER 3   USE OF ENGLISH (1 hour 15 minutes)

For questions **1–15**, *read the text below and decide which answer* **A, B, C** *or* **D** *best fits each space. There is an example at the beginning* (**0**).
Mark your answers **on the separate answer sheet.**

Example:

0	**A** ever	**B** once	**C** only	**D** never

0	A	B	C	D

FAMILY HISTORY

In an age when technology is developing faster than **(0)** .... before, many people are being **(1)** .... to the idea of looking back into the past. One way they can do this is by investigating their own family history. They can try to **(2)** .... out more about where their families came from and what they did. This is now a fast-growing hobby, especially in countries with a **(3)** .... short history, like Australia and the United States.

It is **(4)** .... thing to spend some time **(5)** .... through a book on family history and to take the **(6)** .... to investigate your own family's past. It is **(7)** .... another to carry out the research work successfully. It is easy to set about it in a disorganised way and **(8)** .... yourself many problems which could have been **(9)** .... with a little forward planning.

If your own family stories tell you that you are **(10)** .... with a famous character, whether hero or criminal, do not let this idea take over your research. Just **(11)** .... it as an interesting possibility. A simple system **(12)** .... collecting and storing your information will be adequate to start with; a more complex one may only get in your **(13)** .... . The most important thing, though, is to **(14)** .... started. Who knows what you **(15)** .... find?

1 **A** pushed   **B** attracted   **C** fetched   **D** brought

2 **A** lay   **B** make   **C** put   **D** find

3 **A** fairly   **B** greatly   **C** mostly   **D** widely

4 **A** a   **B** one   **C** no   **D** some

5 **A** seeing   **B** moving   **C** going   **D** living

6 **A** idea   **B** plan   **C** purpose   **D** decision

7 **A** quite   **B** just   **C** more   **D** even

8 **A** produce   **B** cause   **C** build   **D** create

9 **A** missed   **B** lost   **C** avoided   **D** escaped

10 **A** connected   **B** joined   **C** attached to   **D** related to

11 **A** treat   **B** control   **C** contact   **D** direct

12 **A** with   **B** by   **C** for   **D** through

13 **A** track   **B** path   **C** road   **D** way

14 **A** get   **B** appear   **C** be   **D** feel

15 **A** should   **B** might   **C** ought   **D** must

PART 2

*For questions **16–30**, read the text below and think of the word which best fits each space. Use only **one** word in each space. There is an example at the beginning (**0**).*

*Write your word **on the separate answer sheet**.*

Example: | 0 | *to* | | 0 | ‾‾ |

WRITING A STORY

Where do you start if you want **(0)** …. write a successful story? Clearly, what you need first of **(16)** …. is an idea which you can develop into a strong plot. But **(17)** …. do ideas like this come from? The **(18)** …. is 'anywhere and everywhere'. They may come from something that has **(19)** …. to you or to **(20)** …. else, from a newspaper, an interesting picture, or even a song. It's a good idea to keep a notebook nearby **(21)** *so* …. that you can write down the details of any odd incidents **(22)** …. catch your imagination. Make a note of ideas **(23)** …. titles too, and any special phrases or descriptions that you think of. A small tape recorder can **(24)** …. useful for this purpose. Some writers even keep **(25)** …. by their bed in **(26)** …. they wake up with the 'idea of the century'.

Another method of developing the story is to make use **(27)** …. the characters themselves. Why not **(28)** …. putting three people you know well into a situation such as a wedding, where feelings may be very strong, and see **(29)** …. happens. But don't make the final characters too much like your Aunt Jane or Uncle Jim or you may find **(30)** …. in real trouble.

PART 3

For questions 31–40, complete the second sentence so that it has a similar meaning to the first sentence, using the word given. **Do not change the word given.** *You must use between two and five words, including the word given. There is an example at the beginning (0).*
Write **only** *the missing words* **on the separate answer sheet.**

Example:

0 The tennis star ignored her coach's advice.
~~attention~~

The tennis star didn't .... her coach's advice.

The gap can be filled by the words 'pay any attention to' so you write:

0	*pay any attention to*	0	0 1 2

---

31 No one has explained why our flight is delayed.
reason

No one has .... the delay to our flight.

32 I'd rather you didn't phone me at work.
prefer

I'd .... me at work.

33 When Mary wanted a new car, she had to save up for a year.
Mary

It .... save up to buy a new car.

34 They are letting David out of hospital next week.
released

David .... hospital next week.

35 'Did you leave a tip for the waiter, Dad?' I asked.
he

I asked my father .... a tip for the waiter.

36 Jane didn't expect to win the competition, but she entered it anyway.
went

Jane didn't expect to win the competition, but she .... it anyway.

37 I do not intend to tell you my plans.
intention

I .... you my plans.

38 Don't sign for the parcel until you have checked that everything is there.
you

Make sure that nothing is .... sign for the parcel.

39 Sasha only moved to a new class because her teacher recommended it.
Sasha

If her teacher hadn't recommended it, ... to a new class.

40 The motor in this machine needs cleaning once a week.
has

The motor in this machine .... once a week.

PART 4

*For questions **41–55**, read the text below and look carefully at each line. Some of the lines are correct, and some have a word which should not be there. If a line is correct, put a tick (✓) by the number **on the separate answer sheet**. If a line has a word which should **not** be there, write the word **on the separate answer sheet**. There are two examples at the beginning (**0** and **00**).*

Examples:

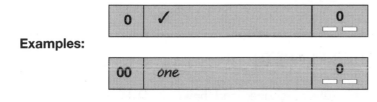

A FAULTY PURCHASE

Dear Sir

0	I am writing to complain about the condition of the cassette
00	recorder which one I bought from your shop on Tuesday,
41	3rd March. Although the outer box it was in perfect
42	condition, I found when I arrived home that the player by
43	itself had obviously been used before and had the
44	several scratches on its case. The headphone cable was
45	badly twisted and I do not think so it will be long before the
46	headphones themselves go out of their shape altogether.
47	In addition, neither of the two free cassettes which came
48	up with the machine was at the beginning. I am sure they
49	must have been being played before by a previous customer,
50	or perhaps the machine had then been used for demonstration
51	purposes. Since there is nothing wrong with the sound quality
52	of the player, but, as I had paid full price, I have a right to expect
53	to receive a brand new equipment. I would therefore be grateful
54	if you would replace for the player with a new model of the
55	same type. I look forward to hearing from you in due course.
	Yours faithfully

*For questions **56–65**, read the text below. Use the word given in capitals at the end of each line to form a word that fits in the space in the same line. There is an example at the beginning (0). Write your word **on the separate answer sheet**.*

Example:

0	*outer*	0

LIFE ON OTHER PLANETS

Humans have long been fascinated by **(0)** .... space, and have wondered if there are intelligent life-forms **(56)** .... , which we might be able to contact. **(57)** .... , we've all seen space creatures on our TV and cinema screens, but 'aliens' like these owe more to the **(58)** .... of using human **(59)** .... to play the parts than to any real form of **(60)** .... investigation.

OUT
ELSE
NATURE
CONVENIENT
ACT
SCIENCE

However, many serious space **(61)** .... are now beginning to turn their attention to the question of what alien life might **(62)** .... look like. One early result is Arnold the Alien, **(63)** .... by biologist, Dougal Dixon. This strange being, **(64)** .... humans, has its eyes, ears and limbs in groups of three instead of pairs but, despite its odd **(65)** .... , its behaviour is not very different from our own.

RESEARCH
ACTUAL
DESIGN
LIKE
APPEAR

PAPER 4   LISTENING (approximately 40 minutes)

PART 1

You will hear people talking in eight different situations.
For questions 1–8, choose the best answer A, B or C.

1   You hear someone introducing a programme on the radio.
Where is he?

   A   a swimming pool

   B   a sports hall

   C   a football ground

                                                            1

2   You hear this girl talking to her mother.
What plan had her mother agreed to?

   A   visiting a friend

   B   going to London

   C   staying in a hotel

                                                            2

3   You hear this advertisement for a concert.
What is unusual about it?

   A   It's on a Saturday.

   B   It's in a different place.

   C   There will be singers in it.

                                                            3

4   You hear this woman talking about herself.
What does she feel?

   A   regret

   B   pride

   C   satisfaction

                                                            4

5 Listen to this man on the phone.
    Why is he calling?

    A to apologise for being late

    B to report escaped animals

    C to offer his help

                                                    5

6 You hear this reporter on the television.
    Who is he going to talk to?

    A a businessman

    B a politician

    C a shopper

                                                    6

7 This boy is talking about something he's been working on.
    What is it?

    A a garden

    B a water sports centre

    C a nature reserve

                                                    7

8 You hear this woman talking to someone outside a block of flats.
    What is her job?

    A She sells property.

    B She is a tourist guide.

    C She inspects building work.

                                                    8

PART 2

You will hear two radio presenters talking about some of the programmes for the coming month.
For questions 9–18, complete the information. You will need to write a word or a short phrase.

Monday 6th
Elton John talking about his
| | 9 |

Wednesday 8th
Win a prize by guessing name of the
| | 10 |

Thursday 9th
Sez U's visit to
| | 11 |

Friday 17th
Report from US on lifestyle of
| | 12 |

Monday 20th
How to save money by using
| | 13 |

Friday 24th
Programme about children of former
| | 14 |

Monday 27th
Music from
| | 15 |

Competition prize
| | 16 |

Tuesday 28th
Report from
| | 17 |

Wednesday 29th
New fashions for people who go
| | 18 |

PART 3

You will hear five people talking about the jobs they'd like to have.
For questions **19–23**, *choose from the list* **A–F** *what they describe. Use the letters only once. There is one extra letter which you do not need to use.*

This person would like to be:

A   a journalist

B   a hotel receptionist

C   a garden designer

D   a nurse

E   a chemist

F   a sales assistant

Speaker 1	19
Speaker 2	20
Speaker 3	21
Speaker 4	22
Speaker 5	23

PART 4

You will hear a conversation between a father, a mother and their son.
For questions 24–30, decide who expresses each idea and mark F for the father,
M for the mother and S for the son.

24 Who admires the action of some neighbours? | 24

25 Who suggests the neighbours are foolish? | 25

26 Who dislikes the place where they live? | 26

27 Who has practical objections to moving? | 27

28 Who explains someone else's idea? | 28

29 Who hopes to be invited by the neighbours? | 29

30 Who believes the neighbours are showing off? | 30

PAPER 5   SPEAKING (approximately 15 minutes)

Part 1

You tell the examiner about yourself. The examiner may ask you questions such as: Where are you from? How do you usually spend your free time? What are your plans for the future? Your partner does the same.

Part 2

The examiner gives you two pictures to look at and asks you to talk about them for about a minute. Your partner does the same with two different pictures.

Part 3

The examiner gives you a photograph or drawing to look at with your partner. You are asked to solve a problem or come to a decision about something in the picture. For example, you might be asked to decide which of two rooms should be used as a study area and which as a leisure area. You discuss the problem together.

Part 4

You are asked more questions connected with your discussion in Part 3. For example, you may be asked to talk about the best ways of studying.

Practice Test 2

PAPER 1 READING (1 hour 15 minutes)

You are going to read a magazine article about a sportsman who is a champion hurdler. Choose the most suitable heading from the list (A–I) for each part (1–7) of the article. There is one extra heading which you do not need to use. There is an example at the beginning (0).

Mark your answers **on the separate answer sheet**.

A	A regular practice routine
B	Concern about the future
C	Not enough time in the day
D	Doing better than ever
E	International living
F	The daily routine varies
G	Home and work
H	Impatience sometimes wins
I	What I eat

My kind of day

| 0 | *I* |

Sometimes I don't eat for a couple of days – it's a personal thing that's developed over the past few years. It seems to me that people often eat out of habit, not because they're hungry. I'll often have a low-fat yoghurt in the morning and sometimes turkey or pasta in the evening.

| 1 | F |

Home is a four-bedroom detached house in Rhoose in the Vale of Glamorgan, near Cardiff, where I was born. I also have a condominium in Toronto, a flat in Richmond, Surrey, where my sister Suzanne lives, and a house in Florida, which is where I train in the winter. My friend Mark McKoy, the Olympic 110 metres hurdles champion, encouraged me to get a place in Toronto and I love it there. It's where I'd like to end my days.

| 2 | G |

My father Ossie, a retired sales supervisor, and my mum Angela, a nurse, live with me in Rhoose but I have my own office where I work for Nuff Respect, the sports marketing and PR company that I run with my friend Linford

Christie. The name comes from a street expression that kids often say to us, meaning congratulations, our respect goes out to you.

3

I'm up about 8am and in training by 10am. Most days in the summer, I go to Cardiff Athletics Stadium with my hurdles partner Paul Gray. I usually drive into Cardiff in my Toyota Supra, pick up Paul and go to the track. We put the hurdles up – glamorous life, isn't it? – do an hour of stretching exercises and get into the hurdles work.

4

Hurdling is a natural thing – I think you have to be born with it. You need to combine a runner's speed with a dancer's grace. Getting technically more efficient is the only way to keep improving and I'm in excellent shape at the moment. I'm confident I can break my 110 metres hurdles world record this summer – in Zurich on 17 August, in Brussels two days later or at the Commonwealth Games on 22 August. There could even be three new world records in a week. Then I'll be focusing on the next Olympics.

5

In the afternoon I do some work for Nuff Respect, using my computer and fax machine. I enjoy the work – after all, I'm the product being marketed – but I have a severe problem with unprofessional people. Usually I'm quite relaxed, but I'll shout at those who waste my time.

6

When the work's finished, I'll shower, change, ask my father what he's doing and maybe pick up Mum from University Hospital. Later, I may drop into Paul's house and cook for him and his family. I cook whatever's there – it's the only artistic thing I do. But I rarely eat it myself.

7

Back home, I'll watch late-night television until I feel tired. I always go to sleep thinking about what the next day holds. Sometimes it seems like a circus, a fantasy world. All I can do is run fast – is that a real kind of world? It certainly won't last forever.

*You are going to read the beginning of a short story. For questions **8–14**, choose the answer (**A**, **B**, **C** or **D**) which you think fits best according to the text. Mark your answers **on the separate answer sheet**.*

I LIVED WITH Mother in a large white house surrounded by tall trees. It was a long walk to the nearest buildings as we were beyond the outskirts of town. It seems to me now that I would ask myself whether we needed to live as we did, she in this lonely white house leading her life, me elsewhere in that same large house, being me. Her child. I suppose in all those years I may have asked myself that, and yet I suspect, in reality, I scarcely gave it any thought.

One day, soon after my thirtieth birthday, Mother told me that she had sold the house. She had found somewhere else, she said. She did not mention where. I did not ask.

Shortly after, two very willing removal men arrived with an orange van which they promptly began loading up with furniture and boxes. Mother directed them from the house. I stood outside underneath our tall trees and watched, fascinated by the process. Many of the things which these strangers were steadily lifting up and taking away had never been moved before in all my lifetime. Indeed, until that moment, I don't think it ever occurred to me that these things could actually be moved. The house and everything in it had seemed so completely fixed. When I saw that the van was nearly full I went indoors to find Mother.

'Keep anything you like,' she said to me. 'I've taken all I want.'

'Thank you,' I said.

'The new people should be here tomorrow.' She climbed into the van alongside the two men, the engine started and they drove away.

Next day, as Mother said they would, a couple came. They were obviously a bit annoyed to find me there. I packed some necessities into a small brown leather suitcase that I did not know was still in the house until I found it. I felt them watch me as I walked away down the path and along the road that eventually led to the railway station.

It had been a long quiet walk so I was surprised when I found the station busy with activity. I had expected to sit for a while and calmly decide my next course of action but a quick glance round the station told me that queuing for a ticket was the first thing for all newcomers to do – buying a cup of tea and trying to find a seat on the platform the next. The queue was long and appeared to move forward only slowly. All well and good, I thought, taking my place behind a woman who was engaged in a fierce argument with her husband while trying to keep several children in order.

'Everyone!' he repeated sarcastically. The husband looked angrily around and as I stood up he caught my eye. I was now part of the argument against him.

'Yes, everyone – so you might just as well make up your mind to enjoy yourself, Harold.'

'I certainly will!' Harold spat back. 'And it won't be with you either!' he told his wife. It was all very public and rather shocking.

'Where to?' The family had reached the front of the queue.

'Two and three halves, returns to Southpool,' the woman declared. Harold was called upon to pay. This he did by counting out the money as slowly as it is possible to count out money. The queue heaved impatiently.

'Where to?'

'Southpool,' I said without a moment's hesitation.

'One way, or are you coming back?' he asked.

'One way,' I said. I was almost surprised when he handed me the ticket. When I had paid, I had half an hour to wait and enough money for a cup of tea. During that half hour, I reckoned it like this: All these people going to the seaside would be eating teas in little cafés along the sea front. Other people would be employed to serve those teas.

The train was packed. I was lucky and managed to squeeze myself on to a seat. I did not see Harold and his family again.

8 When the author was a child, how did she feel about her mother's coldness?
  A She wished her mother were different.
  B She didn't let it bother her.
  C She tried to change their lives.
  D She wondered if she was really her mother.

9 What does 'it' in line 11 refer to?
  A the way she treated her mother
  B the town
  C the way they lived
  D the house

10 How did the author feel when she watched their things going into the van?
  A surprised at how easily their home was taken apart
  B worried about what was going to happen
  C glad her mother was going
  D concerned that the men should do their job properly

11 The author was still in the house when the new people came because she
  A didn't want to go with her mother.
  B hadn't arranged to leave until the day after her mother.
  C hadn't made any plans.
  D didn't want to leave the house.

12 Why did she buy a ticket as soon as she got to the station?
  A because there was nowhere to sit down
  B because she was in a hurry to catch her train
  C because that was what everyone else was doing
  D because she wanted to get away from the crowd

13 Why did she disapprove of the family?
  A because they did not have much money
  B because the children were badly behaved
  C because they did not speak to her
  D because they were arguing in front of other people

14 Why did she feel she had chosen the right place to go?
  A because she hadn't been to Southpool before
  B because she thought she could get a job in Southpool
  C because she was looking forward to having tea by the sea
  D because she couldn't afford to go further

*You are going to read a magazine article about sand. Eight sentences have been removed from the article. Choose from the sentences (**A–I**) the one which fits each gap (**15–21**). There is one extra sentence which you do not need to use. There is an example at the beginning (**0**).*
*Mark your answers **on the separate answer sheet**.*

Sands of time

Sand: as children we play on it and as adults we relax on it. It is something we complain about when it gets in our eyes on a windy beach, and praise when it is made into sand castles. **0** | *I* | If we did, we would discover an account of a geological past and a history of sea life that goes back thousands and, in some cases, millions of years.

Sand covers not just seashores, but also ocean beds, deserts and mountains. **15** | | And it is a major element in manufactured products too – concrete is largely sand, while glass is made of little else. **16** | | Well, it is larger than fine dust and smaller than shingle. In fact, according to the most generally accepted scheme of measurement, grains can be called sand if their diameter is greater than 0.06 of a millimetre and less than 0.6 of a millimetre.

Depending on its age and origin, a particular sand can consist of tiny stones or porous grains through which water can pass. **17** | | They have come from the breaking down of rocks, or from the dead bodies of sea creatures, which collect on the bottom of the oceans, or even from volcanic eruptions.

18 | | If it is a dazzling white, its grains may come from nearby coral, from crystalline quartz rocks or from gypsum, like the white sand of New Mexico. On Pacific Islands, jet black sands form from volcanic minerals. Other black beaches are magnetic and are mined for iron ore.

19 [ ] It washes rock into streams and rivers and down to the sea, leaving behind softer materials. By the time it reaches the sea, the hardest rocks remain but everything else has been broken into tiny particles of 0.02 millimetre diameter or less. The largest pieces fall to the bottom quickly, while smaller particles float and settle only slowly in deeper water, which is why the sandy beach on the shoreline so often turns to mud further out.

20 [ ] If the individual fragments still have sharp edges, you can be sure they were formed fairly recently. This is the case on the island of Kamoama in Hawaii, where a beach was created after a volcanic eruption in 1990. Molten lava spilled into the sea and exploded into glassy droplets.

It seems that when the poet William Blake saw infinity in a grain of sand he was not far wrong. Sand is an irreplaceable industrial ingredient which has many uses. **21** [ ] Sand cushions our land from the force of the sea, and geologists say it often does a better job protecting our shores than the most advanced coastal technology.

A These may have the shape of stars or spirals, their edges rough or smooth.

B It is one of the most common substances on earth.

C In addition, it has one vital function which you might never even notice.

D Rain is an important force in the creation of beaches.

E In the great slow cycle of the earth, sand that was once rock can turn to rock again.

F What exactly is sand?

G Colour is another clue to the origins of sand.

H It can be difficult to date the sand on a beach accurately but it is possible to get a general idea of whether or not the sand is 'young' or 'old'.

I But we don't often look at it.

PART 4

*You are going to read a magazine article about television programmes. For questions **22–35**, choose from the programmes (**A–F**). There is an example at the beginning (**0**).*
*Mark your answers **on the separate answer sheet**.*

Which programme:

gives you recipes from different parts of the world every week?	**0**	*A*
is set in different places?	**22**	
is aimed at beginners?	**23**	
may soon be shown more frequently?	**24**	
involves the presenter's family?	**25**	
tells you about things that can go wrong?	**26**	
contains nothing about cookery?	**27**	
gives information about food production?	**28**	
advises on healthy eating?	**29**	
regularly invites another professional to appear with the presenter?	**30**	
will not continue after its present series?	**31**	
has been critical of some cookery experts?	**32**	
cannot be seen in every television area at the moment?	**33**	
looks at different ways of using one particular food?	**34**	
is very thorough in its research?	**35**	

March's food, health and fitness on the box

A FOOD FILE

Food File tells you exactly what goes into the food on your plate, as the programme follows it from farmyard to factory and finally to your front door. Nutritionist Amanda Ursell returns on Wednesday to present a third series of the popular programme that leaves no lid unlifted and no dishcloth unturned. Last time she told us about the killer bug that lives in hamburgers, asked why we don't always get a good deal from restaurants, complained about cookery writers whose recipes don't work and told us about a new approach to dieting. Plus, there are recipes from around the world as a regular feature.

B YOU CAN COOK

Who can bone a chicken in 30 seconds or less, create a Chinese banquet before your eyes and tell you all there is to know about Asian cuisine? Yan can! Chinese-American chef Martin Yan – cookery teacher, cookbook author and host of the hit ITV afternoon series *You Can Cook* – has been seen on nearly all the ITV regions in recent years. Just lately he's been seen once a week in the Anglia and Central regions. If he isn't on your screen right now, he soon will be again. Martin is seen preparing dishes with an Oriental touch, assisted each week by a different guest such as San Francisco Thai cooking expert Joyce Jue or sausage expert Bruce Aidells. Even his mother and his uncle get in on the act.

C HEALTHWATCH

Latest ideas on the health front are the subject of this new monthly programme which began in December as part of Sky News and is now likely to go fortnightly. The series kicked off with reports on noise pollution, doctors who leave Britain, eye surgery, hospital waiting lists and predicting heart attacks by computer. Presenter Nicola Hill recently introduced another welcome idea from the medical hotline – doctors who prescribe exercises instead of drugs.

D A TASTE OF AFRICA

Presenter Dorinda Hafner cooks nesting pigeons – a favourite recipe from her childhood – when she visits Egypt for her Channel 4 series. Continuing on Wednesdays until March 23, the programme takes viewers to Tanzania for a four-course meal featuring bananas in every course, plus banana wine to wash it down, and to Zanzibar where visitors can try a lipstick straight from the lipstick tree. In Mali, Dorinda visits the River Niger to see the hippo, the country's national symbol, and cook a fine freshwater fish, the capitaine. And there's another series to come later in the year.

E SIMPLY DELICIOUS

Chef Darina Allen has been running her half-hour cookery programmes every weekday at 9 am throughout February on The Learning Channel, covering dishes for family and friends, fish meals and French and Italian food. The final series continues until March 4 with specialities like *bœuf bourguignon* from France and *tiramisu* from Italy, with instructions for people who have never cooked a thing in their lives.

F FOOD AND DRINK

Chefs, wine tasters and other specialists gather together for another round-up of recipes, food news, drinks tips and product tastings. Water prices, wine in pubs, the dangers of dieting and ways of eating to prevent heart disease and minimise the effects of smoking are some of the topics covered so far in this series.

PAPER 2   **WRITING** (1 hour 30 minutes)

PART 1

*You **must** answer this question.*

1   You and your friends have just finished a course and you want to arrange a party. You've had a meeting and made a list of your requirements. You've heard that your friends, Anna and Jack, who attend a nearby school, had a party on a boat last term and you want to ask them all about it.

Read your notes carefully. Then write to Anna and Jack telling them what you want to do and asking for information and advice.

<u>Requirements</u>

20 (30?) people

Begins 9 pm

Cold food/drinks

Dancing!

BOAT??

<u>Ask Anna and Jack</u>
Numbers?
Transport to river?
Food?
Music?
How much? Worth it?
Their opinions?

Write a **letter** of between **120–180** words in an appropriate style on the next page. Do not write any addresses.

PART 1

PART 2

*Write an answer to **one** of the questions **2–5** in this part. Write your answer in*
***120–180** words in an appropriate style on the next page, putting the question*
number in the box.

2   A student magazine is running a series entitled **Books I have loved**, which
    includes reviews of favourite books by its readers.

    Write a **review** of one of your favourite books, explaining what you like
    about it.

3   Your class has been discussing the importance of possessions. For
    homework, your teacher has asked you to write a composition, describing
    two of your favourite possessions and explaining what each of them means to
    you.

    Write your **composition**.

4

> # Radio LGC ═══════
>
> *We would like to receive short reports from listeners for
> a future series of programmes on travel experiences
> called **My most exciting journey**.*
>
> *Reports must include practical details about the journey
> and describe any interesting incidents which happened
> on the way.*

Write your **report** for the radio programme.

5   **Background reading texts**

    Answer **one** of the following two questions based on your reading of **one** of
    the set books (see p. 2). Write the title of the book next to the question
    number box.

    Either   **(a)** How important to the story is the period in which it is set?

    or   **(b)** Describe a character in the book whom you dislike, and explain why.

PART 2

Question	

....
....
....
....
....
....
....
....
....
....
....
....
....
....
....
....
....
....
....
....
....
....
....
....
....
....

PAPER 3   USE OF ENGLISH (1 hour 15 minutes)

For questions **1–15**, *read the text below and decide which answer* **A, B, C** *or* **D**
best fits each space. There is an example at the beginning (**0**).
Mark your answers **on the separate answer sheet**.

Example:

0   **A** in   **B** of   **C** with   **D** for

0	A	B	C	D
	▬	▬	▬	▬

AN AUSTRALIAN MYSTERY

Interest **(0)** …. undiscovered human-like creatures continues to be widespread.
Everyone has **(1)** …. of the Yeti, and its North American 'cousin' Bigfoot, but since the
last century there have been **(2)** …. of the existence in Australia of another, less
famous creature – the Yahoo. In 1912, a Sydney newspaper **(3)** …. an account by
Charles Harper of a strange, large animal he observed **(4)** …. the light of his campfire:
'Its body, legs, and arms were covered with long, brownish-red hair, but what **(5)** ….
me as most extraordinary was its shape, which was human in some ways, **(6)** …. at
the same time very different. The body was enormous, **(7)** …. great strength. The
arms were extremely long and very muscular.'

Harper continued: 'All this observation **(8)** …. a few minutes while the creature stood
there, as if frightened by the firelight. After a few growls, and beating his breast, he
(9) …. , the first few metres upright, then on all four limbs through the low bushes.
Nothing **(10)** …. persuade my companions **(11)** …. the trip, a fact at which I must
admit I was rather pleased.'

What could Harper and his companions **(12)** …. have seen? Such a creature was
(13) …. in south-eastern Australia in the 1800s, but no specimen was ever obtained
for scientific **(14)** …. , and all we are **(15)** …. with today is an historical puzzle.

1 **A** understood   **B** known   **C** heard   **D** noticed

2 **A** statements   **B** reports   **C** arguments   **D** proofs

3 **A** delivered   **B** typed   **C** declared   **D** printed

4 **A** by   **B** at   **C** with   **D** under

5 **A** marked   **B** struck   **C** touched   **D** knocked

6 **A** even   **B** just   **C** still   **D** yet

7 **A** announcing   **B** pointing   **C** indicating   **D** describing

8 **A** lasted   **B** covered   **C** involved   **D** engaged

9 **A** set back   **B** set up   **C** set in   **D** set off

10 **A** should   **B** must   **C** might   **D** would

11 **A** continue   **B** to continue   **C** continuing   **D** having continued

12 **A** probably   **B** likely   **C** possibly   **D** doubtless

13 **A** referred   **B** mentioned   **C** related   **D** remarked

14 **A** arrangements   **B** designs   **C** plans   **D** purposes

15 **A** left   **B** found   **C** seen   **D** met

*For questions **16–30**, read the text below and think of the word which best fits each space. Use only **one** word in each space. There is an example at the beginning (**0**).*
*Write your word **on the separate answer sheet**.*

Example: | 0 | *it* | | 0 |

FAMILY PHOTOGRAPHS

A family portrait is a valuable picture – **(0)** .... is fun to look at now, it's great for relatives far **(16)** .... , and it will bring back memories in the years to come. Families change quickly as children grow, **(17)** .... don't wait, whatever your position in the family – photograph your family group now, and plan to make this **(18)** .... regular event. Your family album isn't really complete **(19)** .... this record of all of you together.

Getting the **(20)** .... of the family together isn't always easy, and so you will need to plan ahead to be sure **(21)** .... has time to pose. A relaxed, friendly feeling is **(22)** .... makes the picture, and you can't expect people to relax **(23)** .... they're in a hurry to do **(24)** .... else. Make your plans when you're all together and **(25)** .... a cheerful, friendly mood – say, during a meal, and set a time convenient **(26)** .... everyone.

A family portrait takes some technical planning, too. Make **(27)** .... your mind in advance **(28)** .... room you want to use; choose your camera position and check the lighting. If you want to be in the picture, make sure you know exactly **(29)** .... the self-timer on your camera operates. With most cameras, you'll have from eight **(30)** .... twelve seconds to get into the picture after you press the shutter button.

PART 3

For questions **31–40**, *complete the second sentence so that it has a similar meaning to the first sentence, using the word given.* **Do not change the word given**. *You must use between two and five words, including the word given. There is an example at the beginning* (**0**).
Write **only** *the missing words* **on the separate answer sheet**.

Example:

0   The tennis star ignored her coach's advice.
   attention

   The tennis star didn't .... her coach's advice.

The gap can be filled by the words 'pay any attention to' so you write:

0	*pay any attention to*	0	0 1 2

---

31   It would be difficult for me to finish the work by the weekend.
   difficulty

   I .... the work by the weekend.

32   Harry's home is still in Spain, is it?
   lives

   Harry .... he?

33   When Sandra walked out of the meeting, she didn't say goodbye to anyone.
   without

   Sandra left .... goodbye to anyone.

34   You can borrow my bike if you're in a hurry.
   mind

   I .... you my bike if you're in a hurry.

35   Angus rarely takes a holiday.
   rare

   It .... take a holiday.

36 We lost the game because of my mistake.
fault

It was .... win the game.

37 Are you planning to do anything on Saturday?
plans

Do .... Saturday?

38 Tim looks nothing like his father.
take

Tim .... his father at all.

39 The film I saw last week was better than this one.
good

This film .... the one I saw last week.

40 I regret giving Dennis my phone number.
Dennis

I wish .... my phone number.

PART 4

For questions **41–55**, read the text below and look carefully at each line. Some of the lines are correct, and some have a word which should not be there. If a line is correct, put a tick (✓) by the number **on the separate answer sheet**. If a line has a word which should **not** be there, write the word **on the separate answer sheet**. There are two examples at the beginning (**0** and **00**).

Examples:

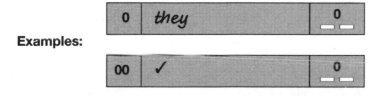

| 0 | *they* | 0 |
| 00 | ✓ | 0 |

THE TROUBLE WITH GOING TO THE CINEMA

0	I don't like the cinema very much myself, but my friends they all
00	love it, and so I often find myself sitting in the dark trying to follow
41	through the conversation on the screen while sweet papers and
42	crisp packets are being opened enthusiastically all around me.
43	It is this sort of annoying disturbance at the cinema which it means
44	that I'd rather prefer to hire a video and watch it at home. Then there
45	is no risk of getting cross because it's impossible to hear anything
46	what is going on. Another problem is that I always do my own best to
47	find a seat with a good view of the screen during the advertisements.
48	Then, at two minutes before the main film is due to begin, the seat in
49	front of me will be taken by a heavyweight boxer who blocks out
50	most of the screen and so, by this time, it's too late to move. I know
51	how this isn't really the point. Cinema fans talk about the extra
52	pleasure of an experience is shared with others. I must admit
53	because there's often a very good atmosphere in the cinema, and
54	I'm probably too sensitive to these things: it only takes up one
55	person making stupid comments to spoil me the whole occasion. On balance, I think I'll stick to my video!

PART 5

For questions **56–65**, read the text below. Use the word given in capitals at the end of each line to form a word that fits in the space in the same line. There is an example at the beginning **(0)**. Write your word **on the separate answer sheet**.

Example:

0	*imperfect*	0

JOB INTERVIEWS

Interviews are an **(0)** .... method of choosing the best people for jobs, **PERFECT**

yet human **(56)** .... like to examine each other in this way. One of the **BE**

many problems of **(57)** .... as it is commonly practised is that the forms **SELECT**

filled in by **(58)** .... often fail to show people as they really are. This **APPLY**

means that you can follow all the best **(59)** .... when completing your **ADVISE**

form and still find that you are **(60)** .... at the next stage – the interview. **SUCCESS**

(61) .... , in the rare cases where interviews are automatic, a candidate **SIMILAR**

with an **(62)** .... form may do surprisingly well. **ADEQUATE**

Of course, your form needs to show that you have **(63)** .... in your **CONFIDENT**

(64) .... to do the job, but don't try to turn yourself into someone else – a **ABLE**

person you have to pretend to be at the interview. Realism and **(65)** .... are **HONEST**

definitely the best approach.

PAPER 4 LISTENING (approximately 40 minutes)

PART 1

You'll hear people talking in eight different situations.
For questions 1–8, choose the best answer A, B or C.

1 This woman is talking on the telephone.
Who is she speaking to?

A her landlord

B an architect

C a builder

	1

2 On holiday, you hear another tourist describing a journey.
How did he feel?

A shocked

B embarrassed

C scared

	2

3 You hear these people talking in a café.
Why did the man change his newspaper?

A the cost

B the opinions

C the quality of the writing

	3

4 This woman is phoning a friend about the date of a meeting.
Why has she called?

A to apologise for changing it

B to inform her about changing it

C to explain the reason for changing it

	4

5 You hear a girl talking about clothes.
What is she describing?

    A a coat

    B a dress

    C a trouser suit

	5

6 Listen to this film critic.
What does he like least about the film?

    A the characters

    B the action scenes

    C the main story

	6

7 You hear these people talking while queuing in a shop.
What does the woman complain about?

    A the payment system

    B the service

    C the quality of the goods

	7

8 You hear these people talking about a book.
Who is the book about?

    A a poet

    B a song writer

    C a journalist

	8

PART 2

You will hear two students who want to be chosen as student representative in their college.

For questions 9–18, complete the notes. You will need to write a word or a short phrase.

Linda wants the college
to offer better advice on _____ **9**

Students need more
information about jobs _____ **10**

She thinks students don't
have enough chances to _____ **11**

She'd like students to
raise money for people who _____ **12**

She wants to
improve the facilities in the _____ **13**

Darren intends to
prevent a rise in the price of _____ **14**

He wants to set up _____ **15**

He thinks the college lacks _____ **16**

He criticises the
way the college handles _____ **17**

He'd like to
invite a greater variety of _____ **18**

PART 3

You will hear five people talking about sport.
*For questions **19–23**, choose from the list **A–F** what they say. Use the letters only once. There is one extra letter which you do not need to use.*

This speaker:

A   has taken up sport as a way of meeting people

B   watches sport in order to relax

C   organises sport for his or her friends

D   organises sport as part of a job

E   does sport in order to keep fit

F   watches sport with friends

Speaker 1	19
Speaker 2	20
Speaker 3	21
Speaker 4	22
Speaker 5	23

PART 4

You will hear a local radio report about places to eat.
For questions 24–30, choose the best answer A, B or C.

24   When should you order a picnic pack from Ali?

   A   by lunchtime
   B   the day before
   C   early in the morning

   24

25   What does Caroline criticise about 'Chick'n'things'?

   A   the quality of the food
   B   the value for money
   C   the speed of service

   25

26   At 'Pat's Café' you are most likely to meet

   A   lorry drivers.
   B   people on walking tours.
   C   commuters.

   26

27   Why couldn't Caroline continue her research after her breakfast?

   A   She was ill.
   B   She wasn't hungry.
   C   She had a long drive home.

   27

28   What did Caroline enjoy at the 'Old Mill'?

   A   the coffee
   B   the cakes
   C   the view

   28

29   What does she mention about the 'Food Box'?

   A   She eats there quite often.
   B   She's a friend of the owner.
   C   She likes to go there on special occasions.

   29

30   What is the problem for customers of the 'Four Seasons'?

   A   Parking is difficult.
   B   The neighbourhood is rather rough.
   C   The staff don't seem to care about the customers.

   30

PAPER 5 SPEAKING (approximately 15 minutes)

Part 1

You tell the examiner about yourself. The examiner may ask you questions such as: Where are you from? How do you usually spend your free time? What are your plans for the future? Your partner does the same.

Part 2

The examiner gives you two pictures to look at and asks you to talk about them for about a minute. Your partner does the same with two different pictures.

Part 3

The examiner gives you a photograph or drawing to look at with your partner. You are asked to solve a problem or come to a decision about something in the picture. For example, you might be asked to decide which of two rooms should be used as a study area and which as a leisure area. You discuss the problem together.

Part 4

You are asked more questions connected with your discussion in Part 3. For example, you may be asked to talk about the best ways of studying.

Practice Test 3

READING (1 hour 15 minutes)

PART 1

*You are going to read an article from a consumer magazine about the London underground railway. Choose the most suitable heading from the list (**A–H**) for each part (**1–6**) of the article. There is one extra heading which you do not need to use. There is an example at the beginning (**0**).*
*Mark your answers **on the separate answer sheet**.*

A	Poor announcements
B	Dirty and outdated
C	Passengers' opinions count
D	Occasional users
E	Overcrowded
F	A waste of time
G	Unreliable
H	Under pressure

THE SERVICE YOU GET ON THE TUBE

0	*H*

THE WORLD'S first underground railway (the Tube) opened in London in January 1863. Today there are 11 lines serving 272 stations, the busiest of which, King's Cross, sees the start and finish of around 70 million journeys a year. But the system is in crisis – mainly as a result of underinvestment. Overcrowding combined with poor reliability can lead to problems for travellers, particularly those who use the Tube during its busiest hours.

1	

This report looks at service and safety on the Underground. It's based on the findings of our survey of passengers. Last June we interviewed 1,698 Tube travellers outside 46 Underground stations in London; 517 regular travellers (those using the Tube throughout the year on three or more days each week) were contacted again and asked more detailed questions by phone.

2	

Since 1981 the number of passengers using the Tube has increased by almost half. The increase in passengers has not been matched by an expansion of the Underground system and there is widespread congestion, particularly during the six peak hours when over 60 per cent of all journeys are made. London Underground Limited (LU) states that over the busiest rush hour no more than one person should have to stand for each seated passenger. But LU's own statistics show that this standard is often not met over large areas of track on a daily basis.

3

Forty-three per cent of regular travellers had missed an appointment or been late for something in the two weeks before the survey because of delays on the Underground.

4

Forty-three per cent of regular travellers mentioned graffiti, rubbish and generally dirty conditions as one of the aspects of the Underground's service they disliked. The aim set by Government for train cleaning is that carriages should be cleaned internally every day they are in use. LU's figures show it has come very close to achieving this. But there are no standards to define or measure how well trains have been cleaned. LU has made progress in dealing with rubbish at major stations but graffiti, old coaches and unmodernised stations remain serious problems.

Well over half of the regular travellers said they were dissatisfied with the information provided when something goes wrong on the system; 72 per cent of those who were dissatisfied complained that the information was wrong or given too late; 49 per cent couldn't hear or understand what was said. LU told us that a new system has been installed, which should mean clearer messages. However, the new system applies only to messages broadcast within stations; those coming from a central control room may not improve for some time to come.

Most of this report reflects the experiences of regular Tube travellers but we also asked those who do not travel every day for their views. The most popular type of ticket bought by these travellers was a one-day pass. Few appeared to have had problems finding their way around the system – 89 per cent said finding their way around was 'easy'.

PART 2

*You are going to read an article about a photographer. For questions 7–14, choose the answer (**A, B, C** or **D**) which you think fits best according to the text. Mark your answers **on the separate answer sheet**.*

Biologically Correct

MY LOVE OF NATURE goes right back to my childhood, to the times when I stayed on my grandparents' farm in Suffolk. My father was in the armed forces, so we were always moving and didn't have a home base for any length of time, but I loved going there. I think it was my grandmother who encouraged me more than anyone: she taught me the names of wildflowers and got me interested in looking at the countryside, so it seemed obvious to go on to do Zoology at university.

I didn't get my first camera until after I'd graduated, when I was due to go diving in Norway and needed a method of recording the sea creatures I would find there. My father didn't know anything about photography, but he bought me an Exacta, which was really quite a good camera for the time, and I went off to take my first pictures of sea anemones and starfish. I became keen very quickly, and learned how to develop and print; obviously I didn't have much money in those days, so I did more black-and-white photography than colour, but it was all still using the camera very much as a tool to record what I found both by diving and on the shore. I had no ambition at all to be a photographer then, or even for some years afterwards.

Unlike many of the wildlife photographers of the time, I trained as a scientist and therefore my way of expressing myself is very different. I've tried from the beginning to produce pictures which are always biologically correct. There are people who will alter things deliberately: you don't pick up sea creatures from the middle of the shore and take them down to attractive pools at the bottom of the shore without knowing you're doing it. In so doing you're actually falsifying the sort of seaweeds they live on and so on, which may seem unimportant but it is actually changing the natural surroundings to make them prettier. Unfortunately, many of the people who select pictures are looking for attractive images and, at the end of the day, whether it's truthful or not doesn't really matter to them.

It's important to think about the animal first, and there are many occasions when I've not taken a picture because it would have been too disturbing. Nothing is so important that you have to get that shot; of course, there are cases when it would be very sad if you didn't, but it's not the end of the world. There can be a lot of ignorance in people's behaviour towards wild animals and it's a problem that more and more people are going to wild places: while some animals may get used to cars, they won't get used to people suddenly rushing up to them. The sheer pressure of people, coupled with the fact that there are increasingly few places where no-one else has photographed, means that over the years, life has become much more difficult for the professional wildlife photographer.

Nevertheless, wildlife photographs play a very important part in educating people about what is out there and what needs conserving. Although photography can be an enjoyable pastime, as it is to many people, it is also something that plays a very important part in educating young and old alike. Of the qualities it takes to make a good wildlife photographer, patience is perhaps the most obvious – you just have to be prepared to sit it out. I'm actually more patient now because I write more than ever before, and as long as I've got a bit of paper and a pencil, I don't feel I'm wasting my time. And because I photograph such a wide range of things, even if the main target doesn't appear I can probably find something else to concentrate on instead.

7 Heather Angel decided to go to university and study Zoology because
A she wanted to improve her life in the countryside.
B she was persuaded to do so by her grandmother.
C she was keen on the natural world.
D she wanted to stop moving around all the time.

8 Why did she get her first camera?
A She needed to be able to look back at what she had seen.
B She wanted to find out if she enjoyed photography.
C Her father thought it was a good idea for her to have one.
D She wanted to learn how to use one and develop her own prints.

9 How is she different from some of the other wildlife photographers she meets?
A She tries to make her photographs as attractive as possible.
B She takes photographs which record accurate natural conditions.
C She likes to photograph plants as well as wildlife.
D She knows the best places to find wildlife.

10 What does 'them' refer to in line 45?

   A sea creatures

   B attractive pools

   C seaweeds

   D natural surroundings

11 Heather Angel now finds it more difficult to photograph wild animals because

   A there are fewer of them.

   B they have become more nervous of people.

   C it is harder to find suitable places.

   D they have become frightened of cars.

12 Wildlife photography is important because it can make people realise that

   A photography is an enjoyable hobby.

   B we learn little about wildlife at school.

   C it is worthwhile visiting the countryside.

   D it is important to look after wild animals.

13 Why is she more patient now?

   A She does other things while waiting.

   B She has got used to waiting.

   C She can concentrate better than she used to.

   D She knows the result will be worth it.

14 Which of the following describes Heather Angel?

   A proud

   B sensitive

   C aggressive

   D disappointed

PART 3

*You are going to read a newspaper article about a family who live on a farm. Seven paragraphs have been removed from the article. Choose from the paragraphs (**A–H**) the one which fits each gap (**15–20**). There is one extra paragraph which you do not need to use. There is an example at the beginning (**0**). Mark your answers **on the separate answer sheet**.*

Ice-cream that keeps the family together

It is a bitter November evening and the westerly winds are howling across south-west England from the Atlantic Ocean. In the warmth of their old stone farmhouse the Roskilly family's thoughts are turned to summer.

0	*H*

'It's a bit unusual but it's worth a try next summer,' says Rachel Roskilly, 59. No-one disagrees with her. Next summer the new flavour of ice-cream will be added to the 33 flavours of ice-cream that the family already produces.

15	

The herd of cows that is the base of the family business is his main activity. There are 90 prime milkers, and 60 calves complete the herd.

16	

Soon after, in 1960, Joe married Rachel. He has added 45 hectares to the farm but has not gone far from his home. 'This year I have not been out of Cornwall,' he said. 'Rachel and I last had a holiday when our son Toby was four. There has just been too much to do.'

17	

'Although we had been making clotted cream since we married and doing holiday lets in the outbuildings for 32 years, we realised that if the farm was ever to support three grown-up children plus their possible families we had to make it a lot more profitable,' Joe said.

18	

'We had decided against ice-cream in 1984 because small-scale equipment was not available at the right price,' Joe said. 'But three years later, when we were looking for a small pasteurising machine with which to make whipping cream, we realised that things had changed.'

19	

In addition, last summer the family opened The Croust House, a 50-seater restaurant serving coffee, cream teas, salads and other light lunches, as well as all the ice-creams and Rachel's home-made bread, scones, cakes and jams.

20	

'Although the cows are the key to everything we do, I have always felt that being ready to change and expand when necessary makes farming more interesting and more fun than it used to be. The younger generation can get bored by the routine of farming. We can keep their interest by bringing in new ideas when otherwise they might have been tempted away from the countryside.'

A Hard work and money have not always gone hand in hand at Tregellast Barton farm. Ten years ago Rachel and Joe were making a turnover of under £50,000 – less than a fifth of what they turn over now.

B Two years ago Bryn, who had gained a degree at the Royal College of Art, was tempted back to the farm by the offer of her own stained glass studio. Toby returned this year from a furniture making course to set up a furniture workshop.

C 'It is very labour-intensive and it is too early to say how it is doing financially,' Joe said. 'But changing the use of some of the cow sheds cost us very little as we did most of the work ourselves.'

D He has been producing milk on the farm, 10 miles from Britain's most southerly point, since he came there to work for his godmother at 17. When she retired she gave Joe the farm of 20 hectares.

E 'Rachel and I invested £5,000 in a pasteurising machine and a deep freeze, convinced that making ice-cream would help keep the children's interest in the farm. It's been very successful.'

F Joe Roskilly, 63-year-old father of the family, sits at the end of the table in his farmer's overalls. He is silent, but under his shock of grey hair he is attentive.

G They looked at ways of making more money from their milk, and also from their Jersey cream, which had a good local reputation. Ice-cream seemed the best idea.

H Halva – the Middle Eastern sweet – is the subject of the conversation. Would it make a good ice-cream flavour? Rachel Roskilly thinks it would. Together with sons Jacob, 31, Toby, 25, and daughter Bryn, 29, she had been experimenting with halva, honey, nuts and their own milk and cream for much of the day.

PART 4

You are going to read a magazine article about different types of guidebooks. For questions 21–35, choose from the books (A–G). Some of the books may be chosen more than once. When more than one answer is required, these may be given in any order. There is an example at the beginning (0).
Mark your answers on the separate answer sheet.

A	Blue Guides
B	Everyman Guides
C	Companion Guides
D	Cadogan Guides
E	Rough Guides
F	Lonely Planet series
G	Time Out series

Which type of guidebook:

is not modern in its approach? **0** C

is attractive to look at? **21** B ✓

offers unconventional views on famous buildings? **22** B E

is not suitable for reading in advance? **23** A ✓

does not help you find your way around a city? **24** G ✓

has a style which might annoy some readers? **25** A E

does not give complete coverage of the sights? **26** D **27** F ✓

takes you on a guided tour of the buildings it describes? **28** A ✓

gives you a personal viewpoint?

| 29 | D |

does not contain what you might at first expect?

| 30 | E |

tells you the history of each building?

| 31 | A |

contains examples of artists' work?

| 32 | A |

is part of an expanding series?

| 33 | D | | 34 | |

concentrates on entertainment?

| 35 | G |

GUIDE to the GUIDES

A guidebook can make or break your holiday. The best will encourage, surprise and delight you, the worst can frustrate and annoy, leaving you lost and bored.

The **Blue Guides** are among the best-known cultural guides. They take you through museums room by room. Their tiny print goes into huge detail to describe the background of monuments that other guides ignore. This is really dull stuff. Curl up in bed with a Blue Guide and deep sleep is guaranteed within two pages. On holiday, however – as you stand curious before a small chapel in a backstreet of Rome – it is the only place to find out everything.

The new **Everyman Guides** cannot compete on detail, but they are a lot more fun. A riot of colour springs from the photographs, illustrations, maps and paintings accompanying the text. Visually they are amazing. In particular the Everyman city guides – such as Prague and Vienna – manage to catch the splendour of their subjects.

Both these series are highly functional, but they lack any real character. Not so the lovingly written, academic and very old-fashioned **Companion Guides**. A day in their company is rather like one spent with your (or at least my) favourite, rather mischievous aunt. Seriousness is always mixed with unexpected and pleasant surprises.

I particularly like the **Cadogan** series, rapidly growing now to cover almost all of Europe. Each one is written by an individual, not a team, which produces generally agreeable personal touches. They will take you down a Parisian side-street to tell you all about a particularly horrible 17th-century murderer or to point out a favourite cake shop. They are all about local colour and most readers will not mind their rushing of museums and missing altogether of lesser monuments.

Rough Guides offer the most successful practical coverage. Their recommendations can rarely be faulted and, as more books come out, their coverage of places of interest gets better. Rough Guides are written in a lively, jolly style about which traditionalists may complain. Prague Cathedral's tomb of St John, described in the Blue Guide as having 'unquestionably the finest furnishings of the time' and thought worthy of a full-page description, is described briefly in the Rough Guide as being a 'work of excess'. I prefer them to their main competitor, the **Lonely Planet** series, which does not even notice the tomb of St John.

The general guides mentioned so far are all arranged in a logical fashion that takes you clearly from place to place. The odd one out is the **Time Out** series. These guides are based on listings: restaurants one after another, shops, museums, nightclubs and so on. For the young, and the young at heart, they are invaluable.

PAPER 2 WRITING (1 hour 30 minutes)

PART 1

*You **must** answer this question.*

1 You have booked a holiday with a travel company, as advertised below, and have already paid in full. Two weeks before you are due to travel, you receive a letter from the company, informing you of changes to the holiday you have bought.

Read the advertisement below, together with the letter from the travel company. Then write to the travel company expressing your displeasure, and explaining why you expect to be given your money back.

Carefree Holidays

Relax in the sunshine at the

Ocean Hotel

☆ Brand new luxury buildings

☆ Olympic-size swimming pool

☆ World-famous chef

☆ Dancing to big-name bands

Dear Sir/Madam,

We regret to inform you that, owing to circumstances beyond our control, building work at the Ocean Hotel will not be completed in time for your holiday. Sports and entertainment facilities will only be available in the second week, and then on a limited basis. Meals will be provided at a nearby restaurant.

We apologise for these changes, but feel sure that you will still have a wonderful time on your Carefree Holiday!

With best wishes

Brian McConnell

Brian McConnell
Carefree Holidays

Write a **letter** of between **120–180** words in an appropriate style on the next page. Do not write any addresses.

PART 1

PART 2

*Write an answer to **one** of the questions 2–5 in this part. Write your answer in 120–180 words in an appropriate style on the next page, putting the question number in the box.*

2   As part of a project on family life, your teacher has asked you to write about a member of your family who has had a big influence on you.

    Describe the person and explain how their actions and character have been important to you.

3   Your local newspaper invites readers to send in short stories about their everyday experiences. The title they have chosen this week is: **Lost and found**.

    Write your **story** for the newspaper.

4   This is part of a letter you receive from a British friend who is studying your language in your country.

> The course is great, but it's a bit formal. Do you have any advice about how to improve my understanding of everyday language? I'd be grateful for any suggestions.

    Write your **letter**, giving details of any newspapers, books, TV programmes, activities etc. you think might be useful and explaining how you would use them. Do not write any addresses.

5   **Background reading texts**

    Answer **one** of the following two questions based on your reading of **one** of the set books (see p. 2). Write the title of the book next to the question number box.

    Either **(a)** Describe the end of the story and say whether you expected the book to finish in that way.

    or   **(b)** Which scene from the book would you choose to put on the cover? Give your reasons.

PART 2

Question	

PAPER 3   USE OF ENGLISH (1 hour 15 minutes)

For questions 1–15, read the text below and decide which answer A, B, C or D best fits each space. There is an example at the beginning (0).
Mark your answers on the separate answer sheet.

Example:

0	**A** ever	**B** then	**C** also	**D** yet

0	A	B	C	D
	▬	▭	▭	▭

LOOK ON THE BRIGHT SIDE

Do you **(0)** .... wish you were more optimistic, someone who always **(1)** .... to be successful? Having someone around who always **(2)** .... the worst isn't really a lot of **(3)** .... – we all know someone who sees a single cloud on a sunny day and says, 'It looks **(4)** .... rain.' But if you catch yourself thinking such things, it's important to do something **(5)** .... it.

You *can* change your view of life, **(6)** .... to psychologists. It only takes a little effort, and you'll find life more rewarding as a **(7)** .... . Optimism, they say, is partly about self-respect and confidence but it's also a more positive way of looking at life and all it has to **(8)** .... . Optimists are more **(9)** .... to start new projects and are generally more prepared to take risks.

Upbringing is obviously very important in forming your **(10)** .... to the world. Some people are brought up to **(11)** .... too much on others and grow up forever blaming other people when anything **(12)** .... wrong. Most optimists, on the **(13)** .... hand, have been brought up not to **(14)** .... failure as the end of the world – they just **(15)** .... with their lives.

1   **A** counted   **B** expected   **C** felt   **D** waited

2   **A** worries   **B** cares   **C** fears   **D** doubts

3   **A** amusement   **B** play   **C** enjoyment   **D** fun

4   **A** so   **B** to   **C** for   **D** like

5   **A** with   **B** against   **C** about   **D** over

6   **A** judging   **B** according   **C** concerning   **D** following

7   **A** result   **B** reason   **C** purpose   **D** product

8   **A** supply   **B** suggest   **C** offer   **D** propose

9   **A** possible   **B** likely   **C** hopeful   **D** welcome

10 **A** opinion   **B** attitude   **C** view   **D** position

11 **A** trust   **B** believe   **C** depend   **D** hope

12 **A** goes   **B** falls   **C** comes   **D** turns

13 **A** opposite   **B** next   **C** other   **D** far

14 **A** regard   **B** respect   **C** suppose   **D** think

15 **A** get up   **B** get on   **C** get out   **D** get over

PART 2

*For questions **16–30**, read the text below and think of the word which best fits
each space. Use only **one** word in each space. There is an example at the
beginning (**0**).*
*Write your word **on the separate answer sheet**.*

Example: | **0** | *their* | | **0** | ⎯ ⎯ |

A BUSY FAMILY

In the front room of **(0)** …. home, the Henry family gathered around their TV set
(16) …. a popular soap opera began. 'Look, there's Mum!' shouted 11-year-old
Kathy, pointing **(17)** …. the screen. 'She's sitting at that table **(18)** …. the corner.'
Sure enough, there was Julia Henry, enjoying a relaxed drink in **(19)** …. of the
country's most famous TV programmes.

Julia's family see **(20)** …. unusual in her job **(21)** …. a 'bit-part' actor, or 'extra',
because they are all doing it. Her husband, Tony, **(22)** …. been in several drama
series as **(23)** …. as numerous adverts, while Kathy and her 13-year-old brother,
Robin, have also appeared **(24)** …. TV countless times.

It all started four years **(25)** …. when Tony, an amateur actor from Lancashire,
decided to leave his job and take **(26)** …. acting professionally. At the age of 41, it
was a big step to take, but he has **(27)** …. regrets about it at all. Soon the whole
family were being offered chances to play small parts just like him, though Tony
admits there are times when he wishes he **(28)** …. a star. 'We really enjoy our lives,'
says Tony, 'although it is difficult to **(29)** …. plans. A couple of phone calls can turn
our week upside down, but we love **(30)** …. minute of it!'

PART 3

*For questions **31–40**, complete the second sentence so that it has a similar meaning to the first sentence, using the word given. **Do not change the word given**. You must use between two and five words, including the word given. There is an example at the beginning (**0**).*

*Write **only** the missing words **on the separate answer sheet**.*

Example:

0   The tennis star ignored her coach's advice.
    attention

    The tennis star didn't .... her coach's advice.

The gap can be filled by the words 'pay any attention to' so you write:

0	*pay any attention to*	0	0 1 2

---

31   I'd rather not spend another day at the beach.
    feel

    I .... another day at the beach.

32   I've never seen a match as good as this before.
    match

    This is the .... seen.

33   The staff in that office all have great respect for their boss.
    look

    The staff in that office all .... their boss.

34   'Is there anything you want from the shops?' Alison asked her mother.
    there

    Alison asked her mother if .... from the shops.

35   Sally might not bring her camera to the party, so I'll take mine.
    in

    I'll take my camera to the party .... bring hers.

36 We missed the turning because we forgot to take a map with us.
remembered

If .... a map with us, we wouldn't have missed the turning.

37 June was sure there were no mistakes in her homework.
nothing

June was sure .... with her homework.

38 Although the weather changed, the picnic went ahead as planned.
spite

The picnic went ahead as planned .... in the weather.

39 I advise you to think carefully before accepting William's offer.
better

You .... carefully before accepting William's offer.

40 Jackie hasn't been swimming for five years.
swimming

The last .... was five years ago.

PART 4

For questions **41–55**, *read the text below and look carefully at each line. Some of the lines are correct, and some have a word which should not be there. If a line is correct, put a tick (✓) by the number* **on the separate answer sheet**. *If a line has a word which should* **not** *be there, write the word* **on the separate answer sheet**. *There are two examples at the beginning (*0 *and* 00*).*

Examples:

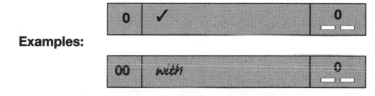

A DIFFERENCE OF OPINION

0	A musician friend of mine once went on an English course during his
00	summer holidays. What he really wanted to do was to improve with his
41	ability to think and react quickly and correctly in the spoken English.
42	He said speaking in a foreign language always made him nervous, even if
43	after three years of study. It turned out so that one of the teachers on the
44	course had very strong views on music, and was not afraid to express
45	them in the lessons. He claimed that music it was a drug, just like alcohol
46	or cigarettes, and people who could not live through their lives without it
47	were to be pitied. Whatever was the subject of the lesson, the teacher
48	always managed to include in some reference to this idea. You can
49	imagine that my friend was not very impressed. In the end, he lost his
50	temper, and spent most of the remaining lessons for arguing about music
51	and its role in people's lives. When his course had finished, he came
52	home still being angry about the experience. However, whether he
53	has enjoyed the course or not, my friend had to admit that the teacher's
54	technique had worked ever since his nervousness in English had completely
55	disappeared and he was speaking far more fluently than before.

PART 5

*For questions **56–65**, read the text below. Use the word given in capitals at the end of each line to form a word that fits in the space in the same line. There is an example at the beginning (**0**). Write your word **on the separate answer sheet**.*

| Example: | 0 | *existence* | 0 | — — — |

THE HISTORY OF TOYS

When did the first toys come into (**0**) …. and what led to their
(**56**) …. ? Did they represent an attempt by adults to make children
happy, or did they arise from the various playful (**57**) …. of children
themselves? As everyone knows, the young (**58**) …. copy the
(**59**) …. of their elders, and, in their play, they often adopt objects
used by adults for entirely different purposes. These objects (**60**) ….
the child's (**61**) …. and lead to games in which everyday articles often
play unusual and (**62**) …. roles.

It is rather surprising that for an (**63**) …. of the origin of toys, we
cannot turn to folk stories. However, no traditional tale (**64**) …. to the
origin of toys exists, and so our (**65**) …. is restricted to archaeological
study and limited evidence from documents.

EXIST
DEVELOP *ement*
ACTIVE
FREQUENT *ly*
BEHAVE *our*
en COURAGE
IMAGINE *tion*
un EXPECT *ing*

EXPLAIN *ation*
RELATE
KNOW *ledge*

PAPER 4   LISTENING (approximately 40 minutes)

PART 1

You'll hear people talking in eight different situations.
*For questions **1–8**, choose the best answer **A**, **B** or **C**.*

1   Listen to these colleagues talking.
    Why is the man going to Amsterdam?

    A   on a business trip

    B   for a short holiday

    C   to study art

2   You're in a shop when you hear one of the assistants talking.
    What is he trying to do?

    A   persuade someone

    B   explain something

    C   correct a wrong idea

3   You hear this reporter on the radio.
    Who is she going to meet?

    A   a fisherman

    B   a scientist

    C   a farmer

4   Listen to this teacher talking to a student.
    What is he giving?

    A   some advice

    B   an opinion

    C   some information

5 You hear this critic talking about an exhibition.
What is its subject?

A life in a city

B the work of an architect

C rich and poor countries

5

6 You are listening to the news on the radio.
Why was Brian Bolter on trial?

A for illegal gambling

B for accepting bribes

C for bribing players

6

7 You are on a bus when you hear this passenger get on.
What does the driver offer to do?

A tell her when the bus reaches her stop

B point out the library

C stop outside the library

7

8 Listen to this boy talking about the town he lives in.
What does he feel about it?

A He likes it.

B It's boring.

C It's old-fashioned.

8

PART 2

You will hear a radio journalist interviewing Frank Irvine, a successful potter.
*For questions **9–18**, complete the notes. You will need to write a word or a short phrase.*

Frank Irvine

Exhibition now at **9** [____] in North London

Early life

Born 1948

Taken to Scotland because **10** [____] was there

As young child mainly interested in **11** [____]

Planned a career designing **12** [____]

Went to Edinburgh to study **13** [____]

Met wife Carole in a **14** [____] in India

His work

At first tried varying the type of **15** [____] which he used

Experimented with high **16** [____] to get unusual effects

In order to produce big images made **17** [____]

Later on made bigger ones for use **18** [____]

PART 3

*You will hear five people being interviewed about how they spend their free time. For questions **19–23**, choose from the list of activities **A–F**. Use the letters only once. There is one extra letter which you do not need to use.*

A   singing

B   walking

Speaker 1	19
Speaker 2	20

C   acting

Speaker 3	21

D   swimming

Speaker 4	22

Speaker 5	23

E   drawing

F   cooking

PART 4

You will hear part of a radio documentary about running a small business.
*For questions **24–30**, decide whether the idea was stated or not and mark **Y** for Yes, or **N** for No.*

24 John believes that some people are incapable of managing a business.

24

25 Sally got advice from her father.

25

26 Megan's business nearly failed.

26

27 John admits that banks may cause problems for small businesses.

27

28 Colin admits that he failed to keep his bank fully informed.

28

29 A chance meeting helped Colin's business.

29

30 John believes that a small business needs a computer to be efficient.

30

PAPER 5 SPEAKING (approximately 15 minutes)

Part 1

You tell the examiner about yourself. The examiner may ask you questions such as: Where are you from? How do you usually spend your free time? What are your plans for the future? Your partner does the same.

Part 2

The examiner gives you two pictures to look at and asks you to talk about them for about a minute. Your partner does the same with two different pictures.

Part 3

The examiner gives you a photograph or drawing to look at with your partner. You are asked to solve a problem or come to a decision about something in the picture. For example, you might be asked to decide which of two rooms should be used as a study area and which as a leisure area. You discuss the problem together.

Part 4

You are asked more questions connected with your discussion in Part 3. For example, you may be asked to talk about the best ways of studying.

Practice Test 4

READING (1 hour 15 minutes)

You are going to read a newspaper article about computers. Choose from the list **(A–I)** *the sentence which best summarises each part* **(1–7)** *of the article. There is one extra sentence which you do not need to use. There is an example at the beginning* **(0)**.
Mark your answers **on the separate answer sheet**.

A	It is uncertain whether computers should take the credit for what they can do.
B	The next computers may operate in a similar way to the human brain.
C	Human beings are no longer necessary in some situations.
D	It is unlikely that computers will ever completely replace human beings.
E	Computers can perform better than a human brain.
F	Computers have more accurate memories than human beings.
G	Human beings and computers use different methods to decide what they should do.
H	There are certain things a computer must be able to do before it can be called 'intelligent'.
I	The expectations of what computers can do have changed over the years.

Unable to think about it

0	*I*

MACHINES which seem to think have become a regular feature of our lives. Tasks that 20 years ago would have been unthinkable are now simple for quite basic computers.

1	

The most complex computers can boast remarkable achievements. Automatic pilots fly jumbo jets, and at the most sophisticated airports such as Heathrow even the largest jets can now land in zero visibility, relying entirely on computers.

2	

Chess is another field where the machine's advances go far beyond mankind's. The most advanced computers are now a match for all but the very best players and it won't be long before they will be capable of beating the champions.

3	

But is it enough for us to describe these machines as intelligent, or are their achievements in reality just a success for the scientists who have programmed them to perform a series of tasks rapidly and efficiently?

4	

Different people use the term 'artificial intelligence' to mean different things. But before it can be argued successfully that we are in the presence of an artificial intelligence, we have to prove that a machine can – as a minimum – 'learn' from the environment, independently of its programmer.

5	

One important difference between computers and the human brain is that computers rely on 'serial processing'. The fact that a computer may be able to win a complex game like chess simply reflects its ability to look at numerous possible series of moves at rapid speed and to 'learn' not to make losing moves. While this does show advanced programming, it does not show that the computer is learning independently of its programming and does not therefore show that it is intelligent. Quite apart from its ability to be influenced by the environment, the human brain differs from even the most advanced computer in that it operates with so-called 'parallel processing', doing several things at once.

6	

Sir Clive Sinclair, one of the original computer experts, is convinced that parallel processing programs for computers will be with us soon, and that these will totally change society. With parallel processing, computers would be expected to 'learn' better from their experiences and perhaps, be able to pass on the fruits of such learning to other computers, each in turn becoming more advanced. Thus could be born a generation of computers able to offer at least a more realistic attempt at intelligence.

7	

Robots are already able to do all sorts of repetitive tasks currently performed by human beings. But the effective control remains with the human brain. No computer has yet been invented which can cope with the details of human language. And the idea of an artificial intelligence with a sense of humour and a conscience still seems a faraway dream. If, however, one was to believe in the faith of scientists working in the field of artificial intelligence, one would have to suspect that dreams just could become reality.

PART 2

You are going to read an article about a famous cook called Delia Smith. For
*questions 8–14, choose the answer (**A, B, C** or **D**) which you think fits best*
according to the text.
*Mark your answers **on the separate answer sheet**.*

TAKE ONE COOK ...

WATCHING HER fingers as they arrange
some greenery on a plateful of pasta in a
London photographic studio, it is difficult to
imagine that there was ever a different Delia
5 *Smith to the confident, no-nonsense*
broadcaster who taught Britain how to feel
good in the kitchen.

Behind the brown-framed glasses, eyes
twinkle with amusement. 'In the early
10 days I wrote the script and learnt it parrot-
fashion – when filming started, my hands
were shaking so much that close-ups were
out of the question.' 'Those early days' were
the first ten-minute afternoon programmes
15 with which the young author of a daily food
column in the *London Evening Standard*
made her first TV appearance exactly 21
years ago this Monday.

Judged not by her personality or
20 entertainment value, but by the test of the
millions of amateurs who copy everything
she does and take in every word, she was to
become queen of TV cooks. An
overstatement? Who else could cause an
25 invasion of the country's chemists, leaving
their shelves empty of liquid glucose, simply
by suggesting it as the secret ingredient of
the perfect chocolate cake? Or single-
handedly create a national shortage of
30 cherry brandy by pouring a drop or two into
a Creole pudding? We've followed her tastes

slavishly, from her preference for freshly-milled black pepper in 1973 to her love for limes in her last book, and Britain's super-markets have responded magnificently.

Such power is impressive. It all began, in the finest traditions of stars-in-the-making, with an eleventh-hour change of mind. Looking for a new cookery presenter back in 1973, the BBC chose an American, Julia Child, but decided she was a touch too transatlantic. Would Delia Smith be interested in taking her place? She popped in, did a ten-minute test programme and waited for the result. Opinions varied, but BBC1 controller Paul Fox liked it and signed her up for the programme *Family Fare*. The budget was so low there was no allowance for film editing. If anything went wrong, the whole dish had to be started again from the beginning.

The TV success continued with a three-part cookery course, *One is Fun!*, then a Christmas series and a series called *Summer Collection*. And as Delia Smith's public acceptance has grown into something not far short of worship, so the suspicions of fellow professionals are less disguised. Who is this popular cook with the boldness to make cooking look easy?

At 54 and with nine television series and an astonishing eight million book sales behind her, she makes no excuses. Cooking, she insists, is meant to be easy. Whenever friends have expressed nervousness about inviting her and her journalist husband to dinner, she always says: 'If I can do it, then you certainly can!'

She has come a long way from the difficulties of her first TV show. She no longer learns the script by heart and now films in a specially-built conservatory in her Suffolk home. So has it all become really easy? 'The light outside keeps changing, planes fly overhead at all the wrong moments and the making of each programme is still very complicated,' she says. 'But I know one thing. I'd far rather cook for television than give a live demonstration. Having a couple of hundred eyes looking at you would be my idea of absolute hell. Whereas doing it for one bored and sympathetic cameraman with his nose in a magazine ... '

8 Delia Smith has become so successful because
- **A** her programmes are entertaining.
- **B** people can actually use her recipes.
- **C** she has an attractive personality.
- **D** she uses unusual ingredients.

9 What does 'It' refer to in line 36?
- **A** her interest in international cookery
- **B** her gift for communication
- **C** the change of mind
- **D** her TV career

10 How did her broadcasting career begin?
- **A** She appeared on TV in America.
- **B** A TV programme employed her as a late choice.
- **C** She helped a famous presenter on TV.
- **D** Her test programme was liked by everyone.

11 What do her fellow professionals think of her?
   A They are ashamed of her.
   B They think her recipes are too simple.
   C They think she isn't a very professional cook.
   D They don't trust her approach.

12 What is her attitude towards cooking?
   A Results depend on the cook's experience.
   B Other people's cooking is more enjoyable than your own.
   C Anyone can cook with the right recipe.
   D You should keep trying if you fail.

13 What does she say about recording programmes today?
   A She prefers recording a programme to cooking in front of an audience.
   B She would prefer to find a television crew who were interested.
   C She misses the facilities which she used at the BBC.
   D She is not as interested in TV presentations as she was.

14 How has Delia Smith changed?
   A She is more relaxed.
   B She is more amusing.
   C She no longer uses a script.
   D She is a better cook.

*You are going to read the introduction to a guidebook about the Yosemite National Park in the USA. Eight sentences have been removed from the article. Choose from the sentences (**A–I**) the one which fits each gap (**15–21**). There is one extra sentence which you do not need to use. There is an example at the beginning (**0**).*

*Mark your answers **on the separate answer sheet**.*

YOSEMITE NATIONAL PARK

WHAT exactly is Yosemite? Is it Bridalveil Fall thundering and pouring in early June? Is it a long summer's day at Tuolumne Meadows? Is it the ice-carved, rocky world of the high Sierra seen from Glacier Point?

| 0 | *I* |

It is an energetic walk over the Four Mile Trail. It is the smell of pine trees at Hogdon Meadow campground. It might also be a walk among some of the largest trees in the world. Our list could go on and on.

| 15 | |

Roaring waterfalls, falling hundreds of feet, fascinate even the most bored traveler. Shining walls of towering rockface challenge the skills of hundreds of mountain climbers and capture the eyes and minds of thousands of visitors. Yosemite's rushing mountain streams, alpine landscape, forests and all the rest of its natural features combine to make this national park unique in the opinion of nearly every observer.

| 16 | |

These earlier inhabitants of the region left traces of a lifestyle which depended upon the use of local plants and animals. Remains of that culture, on display in museums and books, sometimes seen in the surfaces of rock, recalled mainly in names upon the land, show us people's lives which were directly connected to this region.

17 From the earliest Spanish explorers who gave names to the general region, to the fur trappers, miners and others who came seeking paths through the Sierra Nevada or hoping for personal gain, Yosemite displays an exciting past which helps us understand the present. It is a story filled with characters who were impressed enough to stay, advertise, exploit and preserve.

18 Its geologic features are the product of time's hidden forces, carved out by glaciers and streams. Its birds and bears delight suburban America. Its buzzing mosquitoes remind us that we are not in a shopping mall. Its flower-filled meadows and tall forests remind us of the sheep and loggers who once looked out upon this scene.

19 While preserved for all to enjoy, perhaps not everyone can enjoy it at once. Occasionally crowded conditions disturb many first-time visitors. Yosemite Valley does not seem like the quiet place generally shown in photographs. An ever-increasing, demanding public raises the question – can any national park be all things to all people?

20 Bicycling in Yosemite alley, walking the John Muir Trail, skiing at Badger Pass or sitting quietly beside the Merced River are all possibilities. One can walk with freedom in the park, allowing closer examination of the natural surroundings. Alternatively, visitors to Yosemite can take shuttle buses and disembark for short adventures beyond the roadway or can go into informational museums.

Yosemite is a spectacular Sierra Nevada park. Yosemite is history, geology, Indians, scenery beyond compare, and conservation. Yosemite is part of America that we always want to experience and never want to lose. It has become a part of our imagination. We search in Yosemite for what we have not been able to find elsewhere.

21 And that may explain why Yosemite is so popular.

A   Yosemite recalls a history, rich with colorful personalities and filled with dramatic events.

B   Because of that, Yosemite is more than a park, it is an ideal.

C   Yosemite contains natural features which cannot fail to attract human attention.

D   Yosemite is also an example of wild America, in contrast to the America outside its boundaries.

E   For today's visitors, Yosemite offers a source of pleasure and a choice of activity.

F   Yosemite is well-known not just to Americans, but to people all over the world.

G   Yosemite might also be an example of a national park that is too successful, that has become too popular.

H   Yosemite also shows us how the original native American people lived.

I   Obviously, Yosemite is all of these things and much, much more.

PART 4

You are going to read a magazine article about beauty. For questions 22–34, choose from the people in the box (A–G). There is an example at the beginning (0). For question 35, choose the answer (A, B, C or D) which you think fits best according to the text.
Mark your answers on the separate answer sheet.

A	Alfred Linney
B	Mark Lowey
C	Sir Francis Galton
D	David Perrett
E	Francis Bacon
F	Judith Langlois
G	Michael Cunningham

Which person states or stated the following opinion?

A happy expression can be of particular importance.

0	*G*

Some beautiful faces have features which are unacceptable in an ordinary face.

22	

A judgement of whether a female face is attractive or not will vary according to women's position in that society.

23	

Ideas of beauty are not limited by nationality.

24	

When choosing someone for a job, an employer may focus on particular features in a face.

25	

We can recognise a beautiful face when we are very young.

26	

A definition of a beautiful face does not exist.

27	

Making individual characteristics stronger can make a face more attractive.

28	

Features combined from several people are an improvement on individual faces.

| 29 | |

The most beautiful women do not look similar to each other.

| 30 | |

Women who look older are treated with more consideration.

| 31 | |

A face which has completely regular features can never be really beautiful.

| 32 | |

Some features are thought suitable in one situation but not in another.

| 33 | |

Beautiful faces share some of the same types of features.

| 34 | |

35 What is the writer trying to do?
   A explain the different reactions to beautiful faces
   B set out some of the different theories about beauty
   C come to a conclusion about what is a beautiful face
   D explain why people are interested in beauty

Perfect beauty

It's not all a matter of taste – and that's official. But we may be no nearer to learning just what beauty really is.

WE ALL recognise beauty when we see it, but what makes a beautiful face is something that few can agree on. The most controversial finding in some research carried out by **Dr Alfred Linney** of University College Hospital is that there is no such thing as *the* beautiful face. Instead, Linney has found that the features of most top fashion models are just as varied as those of everyone else. 'Some have teeth that stick out, some have a long face, and others a jutting chin. There is no one ideal of beauty that they are all a bit closer to,' he says.

One of Linney's co-workers, orthodontist **Mark Lowey**, even considered that some of the models' features might have required surgery if found on a 'normal' face. 'One type of problem people often seek help for is teeth that stick out,' he says. 'One of the models has teeth that stick out eight millimetres and she still looks lovely.'

Recent findings from UCH go against one of the most influential scientific ideas of beauty – that the combination of the features of several ordinary faces can result in one beautiful face. The theory dates back to the last century and is the work of **Sir Francis Galton**, who made his name both as a psychologist and geneticist. In 1878 he discovered that if photographs of a number of faces were put on top of each other, most people considered the resulting face to be more beautiful than the faces which made them.

But this theory has taken a knock in a recent report from the science magazine *Nature*. **Dr David Perrett**, of the University of St Andrews, combined some photographs of both European and Japanese faces and asked people to judge them. 'We found that not only were individual attractive faces preferred to the combined ones, but that when we used the computer to emphasise the combined features away from the average, that too was preferred,' he said. This would account for the popularity of actresses such as Brigitte Nielsen and Daryl Hannah, who have features that are far from average.

The research also gives scientific respectability to another old idea. As the philosopher **Francis Bacon** put it more than three centuries ago: 'There is no excellent beauty which does not have some strangeness in the proportion.'

Dr David Perrett claims, however, that his beautiful faces had something in common. 'The more attractive ones had higher cheek bones, a thinner jaw, and larger eyes relative to the size of the face than the average ones did,' he says. He also found that beauty can go across cultures: the Japanese found the same European faces beautiful as the Europeans did, and vice versa. According to **Dr Judith Langlois** of the University of Texas, even three-month-old babies prefer beautiful faces to plainer ones.

Another beauty researcher, **Dr Michael Cunningham** of Elmhurst College, Illinois, has been looking at the effect of individual features in a beautiful face and has discovered that some features may or may not be desirable, depending on what the judge is looking for. When male interviewers are selecting a woman for a job, for instance, arched expressive eyebrows and dilated pupils are seen as desirable. On the other hand, men looking for a partner with a view to settling down and starting a family, found a wide smile more important than aggressive eyes and eyebrows. Cunningham also found that attractive women with mature features, such as small eyes and a large nose, received more respect. 'It could be that societies where women have more power and independence idealise women with more mature features,' he says, 'while those which value dependent, weak females may prefer baby faces.'

But the search for a better definition of beauty will continue, driven by the billion-pound beauty industry's desire to find new ways of closing the gap between the actual and the ideal.

PAPER 2   WRITING (1 hour 30 minutes)

PART 1

*You **must** answer this question.*

1   You are in England helping to organise a course for foreign students which begins next week. This morning you received a message from Katarina Tabacek, one of the students who has reserved a place on the course. She wants to bring a friend with her on the course. Look at the description of the course below and the notes you have made and write to Katarina explaining why her friend cannot come on the course.

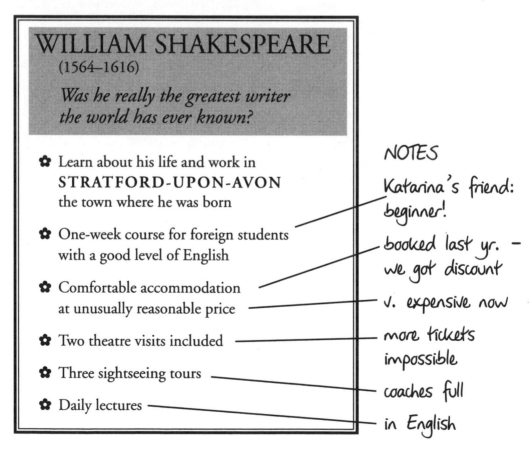

WILLIAM SHAKESPEARE
(1564–1616)

Was he really the greatest writer the world has ever known?

✿ Learn about his life and work in
  STRATFORD-UPON-AVON
  the town where he was born

✿ One-week course for foreign students
  with a good level of English

✿ Comfortable accommodation
  at unusually reasonable price

✿ Two theatre visits included

✿ Three sightseeing tours

✿ Daily lectures

NOTES

Katarina's friend: beginner!

booked last yr. – we got discount

v. expensive now

more tickets impossible

coaches full

in English

Write a **letter** of between **120–180** words in an appropriate style on the next page. Do not write any addresses.

PART 1

PART 2

*Write an answer to **one** of the questions **2–5** in this part. Write your answer in **120–180** words in an appropriate style on the next page, putting the question number in the box.*

2   You have decided to write a letter to a friend or relative while on holiday in a place you have not visited before.

　　Write your **letter**, describing your first impressions of the place and people. Do not write any addresses.

3   Your teacher has asked you to write a short story which finishes with the sentence: **I promised myself there and then that I would never set foot in that place again**.

　　Write your **story**.

4

Television Weekly wants to hear from you!

If the quality of modern television annoys you, here's your chance to let us know why. We'll publish the best articles from readers on the subject: **The problem with today's TV programmes**.

Write your **article** for the magazine.

5   **Background reading texts**

　　Answer **one** of the following two questions based on your reading of **one** of the set books (see p. 2). Write the title of the book next to the question number box.

　　Either　**(a)** Describe any moments in the book which you find especially interesting and say why.

　　or　　**(b)** If you could choose to be one of the characters in the book, who would you choose and why?

PART 2

Question	

....

....

....

....

....

....

....

....

....

....

....

....

....

....

....

....

....

....

....

....

....

....

....

....

....

PAPER 3   USE OF ENGLISH (1 hour 15 minutes)

PART 1

For questions **1–15,** *read the text below and decide which answer* **A, B, C** *or* **D**
best fits each space. There is an example at the beginning **(0).**
Mark your answers **on the separate answer sheet.**

Example:

0   **A** does   **B** do   **C** have   **D** had

0	A	B	C	D

DREAMS

Everyone can dream. Indeed, everyone **(0)** ..A... dream. Those who **(1)** ..D.. that they
never dream at all actually dream **(2)** ..B.. as frequently as the rest of us, **(3)** ..C.. they
may not remember anything about it. Even those of us who are perfectly **(4)** ..C.. of
dreaming night **(5)** ..A.. night very seldom remember those dreams in **(6)** ..A.. detail
but merely retain an untidy mixture of seemingly unrelated impressions. Dreams
are not simply visual – we dream with all our **(7)** ..D. , so that we appear to
experience sound, touch, smell, and taste.

One of the world's oldest **(8)** ..B. written documents is the Egyptian *Book of
Dreams*. This volume is about five thousand years old, so you can **(9)** ..A. that
dreams were believed to have a special significance even then. Many ancient
civilisations believed that you **(10)** ..C.. never wake a sleeping person as, during
sleep, the soul had left the body and might not be able to return **(11)** ..in. time if the
sleeper were suddenly **(12)** ..C.. .

From ancient times to the present **(13)** ..C. , people have been **(14)** ..A. attempts to
interpret dreams and to explain their significance. There are many books available
on the subject of dream interpretation, although unfortunately there are almost as
many meanings for a particular dream **(15)** ..as. there are books.

1 **A** demand   **B** promise   **C** agree   **D** claim

2 **A** also   **B** just   **C** only   **D** quite

3 **A** though   **B** besides   **C** however   **D** despite

4 **A** familiar   **B** accustomed   **C** aware   **D** used

5 **A** after   **B** on   **C** through   **D** over

6 **A** great   **B** high   **C** strong   **D** deep

7 **A** feelings   **B** emotions   **C** impressions   **D** senses

8 **A** considered   **B** known   **C** regarded   **D** estimated

9 **A** see   **B** feel   **C** ensure   **D** think

10 **A** would   **B** ought   **C** should   **D** need

11 **A** by   **B** in   **C** with   **D** for

12 **A** awoke   **B** awoken   **C** awake   **D** awaken

13 **A** minute   **B** hour   **C** moment   **D** day

14 **A** doing   **B** putting   **C** making   **D** taking

15 **A** as   **B** like   **C** so   **D** such

PART 2

*For questions **16–30**, read the text below and think of the word which best fits each space. Use only **one** word in each space. There is an example at the beginning (**0**).*
*Write your word **on the separate answer sheet**.*

Example: | 0 | *is* | | 0 |

THE EXPORT OF ICE

Ice from the Rocky Mountains in the United States (**0**) ..*is*.. being exported to countries on the other (**16**) part. of the world. From Seattle to Tokyo (**17**) ..it. seem a long way to send ice, but the idea is certainly not new. (**18**) As early as 1833, Frederick Tudor, (**19**) known as the 'Ice King', sent a shipload of ice from America to India. About half (**20**) of. ice melted during the long journey, but Tudor would have (**21**) made a profit even (**22**) if. he had lost three quarters of his cargo.

Most people think (**23**) that ice as rather short-lived but, when it was cut from frozen lakes in huge blocks and stored in the depths of a sailing ship, (**24**) his life was considerably extended. In Britain in the 1840s, (**25**) there was already a local commercial ice trade, but the import of ice, first from America and then from Norway, (**26**) did about a revolution in the food business. The main port of entry for Norwegian ice was London, from (**27**) watching the firm of Carlo Gatti, the largest dealers, distributed ice around the country. It was Gatti (**28**) who introduced the penny ice-cream in the 1850s. (**29**) And then, ice-cream had been a luxury, but the penny ice, served in Gatti's cafés, became a Victorian fashion and brought hundreds of Italian ice-cream sellers (**30**) to. the streets of the capital.

PART 3

*For questions **31–40**, complete the second sentence so that it has a similar meaning to the first sentence, using the word given. **Do not change the word given**. You must use between two and five words, including the word given. There is an example at the beginning (**0**).*
*Write **only** the missing words **on the separate answer sheet**.*

Example:

0   The tennis star ignored her coach's advice.
~~**attention**~~

The tennis star didn't .... her coach's advice.

The gap can be filled by the words 'pay any attention to' so you write:

0	*pay any attention to*		0	0 1 2

---

31   Martin hasn't mentioned the party to me at all.
word

Martin hasn't ...*he said a word to* *me* ✓... about the party. ✓   *5*

32   Apparently, Sheila wasn't listening to me.
appear

Sheila ...*wasn't appear of*..... listening to me.

33   Margaret was offered a place on the course but couldn't accept because she was ill.
turn

Margaret was offered a place on the course but ...*turned down*... because she was ill.

34   'I wouldn't trust Frank with your money if I were you, Carl,' I said.
advised   *to trust on*

I ...*advised Carl not*...... Frank with his money. ✗ *1/2*

35   I don't know Lesley's reasons for resigning.
idea

I ...*have no idea why*... Lesley resigned. ✓

36 Have you any desks in stock which are cheaper than this?
    desk

    Is this ...*the cheapest desk*... in stock? ¹/₂

37 Teams of experts were examining the damage to the building.
    examined

    The damage to the building ...*were examined by*.... teams of experts. ¹/₂

38 Joe's father used to insist that he washed the car at the weekend.
    make

    Joe's father used to ...*make washed*........ the car at the weekend.

39 I wish John still wrote to me.
    miss

    I ...*miss letter*........... from John. ¹/₂

40 Everyone thinks Alan will accept the job within the next few days.
    expected

    Alan ...*is expected to accept*... the job within the next few days. ∧

PART 4

For questions 41–55, read the text below and look carefully at each line. Some of the lines are correct, and some have a word which should not be there. If a line is correct, put a tick (✓) by the number on the separate answer sheet. If a line has a word which should not be there, write the word on the separate answer sheet. There are two examples at the beginning (0 and 00).

Examples:

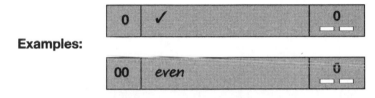

0	✓	0
00	*even*	0̶

IS LETTER-WRITING A LOST ART?

0	Do you write letters any more? In this age of advanced telephone
00	networks and electronic mail, it seems that fewer and even fewer people are
41	taking the time to sit down and write letters to friends and relatives. For
42	hundreds of past years, letters were the only way to keep in touch with
43	people who were at any distance away, and letter-writing was seen as an
44	important skill for all those educated people to master. Gradually, however,
45	the importance of letter-writing has decreased up to a point where the majority
46	of us must have to make a special effort to turn out something worthwhile when
47	we apply for a job or make a complaint. Personal letters, just when we
48	bother to write them at all, are often not much more than a stream of
49	unconnected thoughts. In business circles, the same tendency is for routine
50	communications to become shorter and, although clients they may
51	appreciate a detailed letter, an employee who sends out long letters is often
52	regarded as an inefficient. Many people prefer the telephone in all
53	circumstances and, naturally, its own speed is vital in many situations but
54	how very often have you put the phone down, dissatisfied with what you
55	have managed to say? I don't think I'll throw my pen away from yet.

10

PART 5

*For questions **56–65**, read the text below. Use the word given in capitals at the end of each line to form a word that fits in the space in the same line. There is an example at the beginning (**0**). Write your word **on the separate answer sheet**.*

Example:

0	*painting*	0

A CHANGE OF CAREER

Wildlife **(0)** *painting* .... had always been a hobby for Mark Chester, but when he lost his job, he took the **(56)** .... to turn it into a full-time career. Mark had obtained his **(57)** .... qualifications in the fields of **(58)** .... and advertising and felt that these skills would be useful in his new life. He had sold his work before, and was **(59)** .... confident that he could earn enough to live on.

PAINT
DECIDE *decision* ✓
PROFESSION *al* ✓
PHOTOGRAPH *ing*
REASON *ably* ✓

Mark discovered that he would be able to receive an **(60)** .... from a government **(61)** .... to help him set up his business. They also provided him with **(62)** .... information on how to run his affairs. As **(63)** .... of his work increased, Mark realised that he could not paint enough **(64)** .... pictures to keep up with demand, so he is now trying to interest a **(65)** .... in producing prints of his work. Meanwhile, Mark has started making prints of his own.

ALLOW *ance* ✓
AGENT *agency*
USE *full*
SELL *ing* *sales*
ORIGIN *al* ✓
PUBLISH
publication
published
public
publisher

4

PAPER 4 LISTENING (approximately 40 minutes)

PART 1

You will hear people talking in eight different situations.
For questions 1–8, choose the best answer A, B or C.

1   You hear this man talking on the radio about a politician.
    When did he get to know her?

    A   at school

    B   at university

    C   in his first job

2   You're in a restaurant when you overhear this conversation.
    What is wrong with the food?

    A   It's stale.

    B   It's overcooked.

    C   It's the wrong order.

3   You hear the weather forecast on the radio.
    How long will the bad weather last?

    A   until midday tomorrow

    B   until tomorrow evening

    C   until the day after tomorrow

4   You are in a bank when you hear this conversation.
    What does the woman want to do?

    A   borrow some money

    B   take out some of her money

    C   transfer her money to a new account

137

5   Listen to this man describing a concert.
    What did he like about it?

    A   the first part

    B   the songs

    C   the instrumental section

	5

A.

6   Listen to these language teachers.
    What may cause a problem for students, according to the woman?

    A   violence

    B   prejudice

    C   loneliness

	6

B.

7   Some friends are talking about a film.
    What does the boy emphasise about the director?

    A   She's Indian.

    B   She's a woman.

    C   She's young.

	7

C.

8   You hear this woman talking about a colleague on the phone.
    What has he done?

    A   passed his driving test

    B   bought a car

    C   started driving lessons

	8

A.

Visual materials for Paper 5

1A

1B

1C

1D

1E

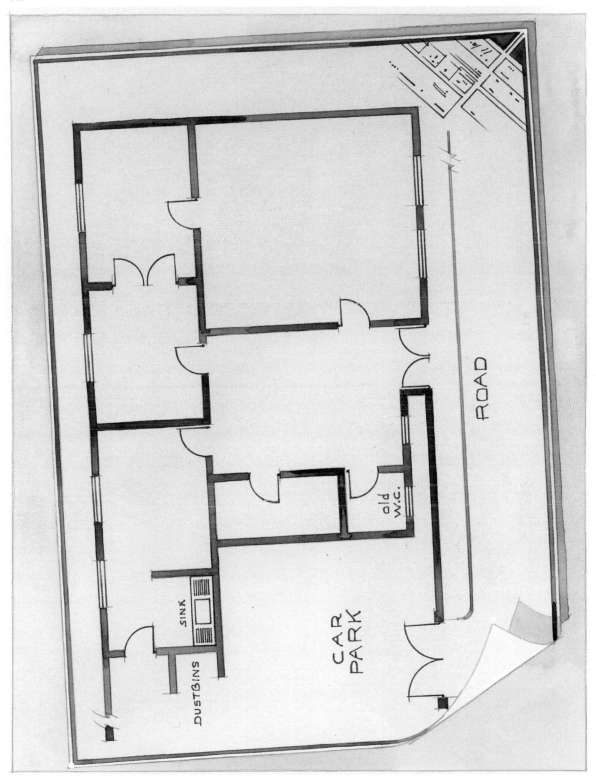

2A

2B

3A

3B

2C

2D

2E

3C

3D

4A

4B

4C

4D

3E

4E

City Football
Holiday Moday 9am–2pm.
Lots of Stalls and Buyers
(Sorry no dogs allowed)

children free. All proceeds to
British Red Cross

LIGHT
IDEAS

Club

ly
and
died.

Save our Swimming Pool

If you want to help, contact:

Workshop
theatre
part of
Develop
East

SAVE OUR
SWIMMING
POOL

MEETING
TONIGHT
8 pm.

SAVE OUR
SWIMMING
POOL

PART 2

You will hear a radio feature about the city of Bristol.
*For questions **9–18**, complete the notes. You will need to write a word or a short*
phrase.

Bristol

Ashton Court

9 [a couple of] miles from centre

Visitor Centre has display about 100 years

of **10** [history] exhibition

Museums

In **11** [ ] area

Industrial Museum

Many examples of things to do with **12** [transport]

S.S. Great Britain

An early ship made of **13** [iron]

Bristol Zoo

Special events include displays, treasure hunts, and an

exhibition of **14** [ ] of wildlife

For little children, there's the **15** [ ]

For bigger children, there's the **16** [ ]

The Exploratory

Opportunity to learn about many aspects

of **17** [ ]

Variety of shows, including 'Bubble Magic'

and **18** [ ]

PART 3

You will hear five people talking about feelings they have experienced.
*For questions **19–23**, choose from the list of feelings **A–F**. Use the letters only once. There is one extra letter which you do not need to use.*

A   guilt

B   anger

C   fear

D   homesickness

E   shyness

F   embarrassment

Speaker 1		19
Speaker 2		20
Speaker 3		21
Speaker 4		22
Speaker 5		23

PART 4

You will hear part of a radio interview with Sharon Walker, a young woman who has recently changed her career.
For questions 24–30 decide whether the statements are true or false and mark **T** *for True, or* **F** *for False.*

24   Sharon gave up professional tennis three years ago. | 24 |

25   She still enjoys playing. | 25 |

26   When she was young, she was amused by newspaper
     reports about her. | 26 |

27   She says that journalists invented stories about her love life. | 27 |

28   She was criticised by some other players when she retired. | 28 |

29   She has been feeling unfulfilled since she retired. | 29 |

30   It's unimportant to her how well Maisie plays tennis. | 30 |

PAPER 5 SPEAKING (approximately 15 minutes)

Part 1

You tell the examiner about yourself. The examiner may ask you questions such as: Where are you from? How do you usually spend your free time? What are your plans for the future? Your partner does the same.

Part 2

The examiner gives you two pictures to look at and asks you to talk about them for about a minute. Your partner does the same with two different pictures.

Part 3

The examiner gives you a photograph or drawing to look at with your partner. You are asked to solve a problem or come to a decision about something in the picture. For example, you might be asked to decide which of two rooms should be used as a study area and which as a leisure area. You discuss the problem together.

Part 4

You are asked more questions connected with your discussion in Part 3. For example, you may be asked to talk about the best ways of studying.

Keys and Tapescripts

Test 1 Key

Paper 1 Reading

Part 1
1 F   2 G   3 A   4 D   5 C   6 E

Part 2
7 C   8 A   9 B   10 D   11 B   12 A   13 C   14 D

Part 3
15 D   16 A   17 G   18 C   19 F   20 B

Part 4
21 B   22 D   23 and 24 B/E   25 B   26 F   27 A   28 C
29 B   30 D   31 B   32 A   33 E   34 A   35 C
(Where there are two possible answers, these are interchangeable.)

Paper 2 Writing

Part 1

Plan

<u>letter to Stephen</u>

thanks for his letter
pleased to hear brother's plan

we had good time
few things should mention
- pools good for all standards
- coach strict – frightened some children
- didn't go on excursions because tired – so much exercise & couldn't sleep because of noisy entertainment

hope my info helps him decide

look forward to next letter

Model answer

Dear Stephen,

Thanks for your letter. It was good to hear from you.

I was pleased to hear your brother is planning to take his family on a swimming course. We certainly learnt a lot at Merle Park. However, there were a few things which we didn't like, so perhaps you should mention them to your brother.

The pools are excellent, whatever standard you are, and the instruction is very professional, but the coach is very strict and some little children were rather frightened of him. Apart from that, it's a very good course. I must admit we didn't go on any of the excursions because we were so tired from all the exercise. Also we didn't get enough sleep as the entertainment in the evenings was rather noisy.

I hope this information is helpful for your brother. I look forward to getting your next letter and hearing what he's decided.

All the best,

Max

(151 words)

Part 2 Question 2

Plan

> <u>my best holiday</u>
>
> why we decided to go
>
> setting up camp – no matches
>
> weather – my memory
>
> plants, birds, etc.
>
> getting to know father

Model answer

When I was nine I read a book about camping and complained to my father that we never did anything like that. My father works in an office and has little spare time, so I was surprised when he said, 'Fine, let's go next week!'

We arrived in the late afternoon and put up our tent. Then we got out our camp stove and frying pan because we were very hungry. Disaster – no matches! We were sadly preparing to eat bread and drink cold water, when my father realised he had some matches in his jacket pocket. We were saved. It was the best meal of my life, even though we burnt the sausages.

It was a wonderful holiday. I remember perfect weather, although my father says it rained twice. We walked every day and my father taught me about plants and the wild birds we saw. I learnt a lot about my father, too, and we have always had a good relationship since that week. That's really why I think it was the best holiday I've ever had.

(180 words)

Part 2 Question 3

Plan

> <u>story</u>
>
> *boss busy – visitor – I check restaurant*
>
> *nice table – free drink*
>
> *next table – couple with restaurant guide – see name on cover*
>
> *All at once… – enjoyed meal*

Model answer

My boss is a very busy man. Three years ago, he was expecting an important customer from abroad. He asked me to try a new local restaurant to see if it would be a good place to take our visitor. Naturally, I booked a table for myself immediately.

When I gave my name to the head waiter he showed me to a table by the window and offered me a free drink while I looked at the menu. I wondered if he was being kind to me because I was eating alone.

At the next table was a young couple. The husband was holding a book. It was a restaurant guide and he was reading the comments in it to his wife. When the waiter brought his bill, the man put down the book and I saw the author's name on the cover.

All at once I began to understand why I was being treated so well. It was the same name as mine! I must admit I really enjoyed that meal.

(171 words)

Part 2 Question 4

Plan

> report about shopping
>
> 3 main places
>
> 1 market – stalls
>   fruit & veg
>   good cheese
>   cheap clothes
>   ★ good atmosphere
> 2 High Street – variety
>   department stores
>   bookshop
>   ★ helpful service
> 3 New Mall – edge of town
>   supermarket
>   fashion shops
>   electrical goods
>   ★ easy to park & get around

Model answer

> Shopping facilities in the area
>
> There are three main places for shopping.
>
> 1 The market
>
> The market is held on Thursdays and Saturdays in the square. Most of the stalls sell fresh fruit and vegetables, but there is also a good cheese stall which is well worth visiting, and several stalls which sell cheap clothing, such as T-shirts. The atmosphere is lively and it is pleasant to wander about, just looking and listening.
>
> 2 The High Street
>
> There are a variety of shops in the High Street including two department stores. The bookshop on the corner has both new and second-hand books and is a great place to pass an hour on a rainy day. The shop assistants are all very helpful.
>
> 3 The New Mall
>
> The Mall is on the edge of town, near the main road. It has a large supermarket and two shops selling electrical goods as well as lots of shops for fashion clothes and shoes. It has a large car park and of course it is easy to walk around inside, whatever the weather.

(176 words)

Paper 3 Use of English

Award one mark for each correct answer, except in Part 3, where two marks are available, divided up as shown, for each answer.

Correct spelling is essential throughout. Ignore omission or abuse of capital letters. No half marks.

Part 1

1 B   2 D   3 A   4 B   5 C   6 D   7 A   8 B   9 C
10 A   11 A   12 C   13 D   14 A   15 B

Part 2

16 all   17 where   18 answer/reply   19 happened/occurred
20 someone/somebody   21 so   22 which/that   23 for/about
24 be/prove   25 one/theirs   26 case   27 of   28 try
29 what   30 yourself

Part 3

31 told us/given/explained the OR given (us) a (1) reason for (1)
32 prefer you (1) not to phone (1)
33 took Mary (1) a year to (1)
34 is being/will be released (1) from (1)
35 if/whether he (1) had left (1)
36 went in (1) for (1)
37 have no intention (1) of telling (1)
38 missing (1) before you (1)
39 Sasha wouldn't (1) have moved (1)
40 has to (1) be cleaned (1)

Part 4

41 it   42 by   43 the   44 ✓   45 so   46 their   47 ✓
48 up   49 being   50 then   51 since   52 had   53 a
54 for   55 ✓

Part 5

56 elsewhere   57 Naturally   58 convenience   59 actors/actresses
60 scientific   61 researchers   62 actually   63 designed
64 unlike   65 appearance

Paper 4 Listening

Part 1

1 A   2 B   3 C   4 C   5 B   6 A   7 C   8 A

Part 2

9 early career   10 (mystery) host   11 (the) Far East
12 (a) student(s)   13 (student) travelcards
14 rock musicians/big (music) names   15 Jamaica
16 trip to Brazil   17 (a) shoe museum   18 dancing (in clubs)/to clubs

Part 3

19 C   20 A   21 D   22 B   23 F

Part 4

24 S   25 F   26 M   27 F   28 S   29 F   30 S

Tapescript   *First Certificate Practice Test One. Paper Four. Listening. Hello. I'm going to give you the instructions for this test. I'll introduce each part of the test and give you time to look at the questions.*
At the start of each piece, you'll hear this sound:

tone

You'll hear each piece twice.
Remember, while you're listening, write your answers on the question paper. You'll have time at the end of the test to copy your answers onto the separate answer sheet.

The tape will now be stopped. Please ask any questions now, because you must not speak during the test.

[pause]

PART 1   *Now open your question paper and look at Part One.*
You'll hear people talking in eight different situations. For questions 1 to 8, choose the best answer, A, B or C.

Question 1   One
You hear someone introducing a programme on the radio. Where is he?
A *a swimming-pool*
B *a sports hall*
C *a football ground*

[pause]

tone

149

Reporter: . . . and I'm here outside now and there's quite a crowd beginning to build up behind the fence. They're hoping to get in to see what the new changing rooms are like – supposed to be really luxurious compared to the old ones – and also the new diving area which I understand is overlooked by the café – should make that a good place to pass the time while you're getting dry. And now here is the Mayor of Taunton arriving to actually perform the opening ceremony . . .

[pause]

tone

[The recording is repeated.]

[pause]

Question 2   *Two*
You hear this girl talking to her mother. Which plan had her mother accepted?
A visiting a friend
B going to London
C staying in a hotel

[pause]

tone

Girl: But you said it was all right.
Mother: That was for the day. You're not wandering about London at night, staying with some friends of Antonia's brother I've never heard of . . .
Girl: We could stay in a hotel.
Mother: That shows just how little you and Antonia know about it. I agreed to a day's shopping and so did her mother. Either you come back on the evening train or you don't go.
Girl: Oh, Mum.

[pause]

tone

[The recording is repeated.]

[pause]

Question 3   *Three*
You hear this advertisement for a concert. What is unusual about it?
A It's on a Saturday.
B It's in a different place.
C There will be singers in it.

[pause]

tone

Announcer: Next Saturday evening the City Symphony Orchestra will be joined for their regular monthly concert, starting at eight o'clock, at the Festival Hall, by singers from the High

School and the City Music Society, for a performance of Beethoven's Ninth Symphony. An occasion not to be missed, I'm sure.

[pause]

tone

[The recording is repeated.]

[pause]

Question 4   *Four*
You hear this woman talking about herself. What does she feel?
A regret
B pride
C satisfaction

[pause]

tone

Woman: I think it's very difficult for people nowadays to imagine how it was for us. We had far fewer choices than girls nowadays. I know I never married, and it wouldn't be true to say I never thought about the pleasures of bringing up children. But on the whole I don't think I'm suited to motherhood. So I've no doubt it was for the best. Anyway – the choice was partly my own and partly just the way things turned out for me – I really don't see any reason to complain.

[pause]

tone

[The recording is repeated.]

[pause]

Question 5   *Five*
Listen to this man on the phone. Why is he calling?
A to apologise for being late
B to report escaped animals
C to offer his help

[pause]

tone

Man: I'm actually on my way to town now . . . no, no, . . . sorry to be the bringer of bad news, but . . . yes, I came down the back road and they're all over the place . . . the hedge is all smashed up. Will you be able to fix something, do you think? . . . I'm really sorry, I just can't – I've got to get to my meeting . . . At least the bull wasn't in there with them! . . . Yeah, okay, I'll probably be round tonight. . . . Sure. See you later.

[pause]

tone

[The recording is repeated.]

[pause]

Question 6 *Six*
You hear this reporter on the television. Who is he going to talk to?
A a businessman
B a politician
C a shopper

[pause]

tone

Reporter: . . . for many years now. They say that the market is no longer needed, as people shop in the suburbs, and it just leads to worse traffic problems. But the fact remains that there's been a market on this spot for hundreds of years and a number of local shopkeepers feel that without it, the city centre will just die. They've got together to make their views known to the authorities. One of them's here with me now. Alan Green, what exactly is it you think should be done here?

[pause]

tone

[The recording is repeated.]

[pause]

Question 7 *Seven*
This boy is talking about something he's been working on. What is it?
A a garden
B a water sports centre
C a nature reserve

[pause]

tone

Teenage boy: We, er, started with just three of us, then I got some other people along, er, from, you know, school and things. We've cleaned up the litter from the grass banks, and fixed, like, a path, with markers, so people don't go too near where the birds nest. We've done a map of, um, the best places to, er, watch them from. There's a sailing club at the other end of the lake, but, er, they've said, we asked them, and they've said they're going to put markers across the water too. So, that'll be a big help.

[pause]

tone

[The recording is repeated.]

[pause]

Question 8   *Eight*
You hear this woman talking to someone outside a block of flats. What is her job?
A *She sells property.*
B *She is a tourist guide.*
C *She inspects building work.*

[pause]

tone

Estate agent: . . . as you can see, the outside of the block is maintained to a high standard, and the gardens are extremely well-designed. This block was built just under a hundred years ago and a number of well-known people have lived here, including poets, artists and writers. Now, if we go up to the flat I want to show you, you'll see that the view across to the castle is really something special. Now, as I mentioned on the phone, these are rarely available, so if you are interested I would advise you to let us know . . .

[pause]

tone

[The recording is repeated.]

[pause]

That's the end of Part One.
Now turn to Part Two.

PART 2   *You will hear two radio presenters talking about some of the programmes for the coming month. For questions 9 to 18, complete the information. You will need to write a word or a short phrase.*
You now have forty-five seconds in which to look at Part Two.

[pause]

tone

Rita: And now I've got with me Greg, who's going to fill us in on some of the special things coming up this month. What've you got for us, Greg?
Greg: Hi, Rita. Yeah, I've got several really special programmes to tell you about.
Rita: And this is retro month here on Intersound, so I guess we'll be looking back quite a bit?
Greg: That's right. And we start with an interview which'll take us back to the music scene in the early seventies – that's Elton John talking about his early career – and we'll be playing some of his favourite early tracks.
Rita: And that's on Monday the 6th?
Greg: At seven-thirty.
Rita: Great. And then on Wednesday the 8th we're going to visit somebody else connected with the seventies, am I right?
Greg: Yes, but I'm not telling you any more, because that's this month's mystery visit, when I talk to someone in their home and listeners have the chance to win a great prize by ringing in with their guesses as to the identity of my mystery host. Now all I'm going to say is that this is someone we associate with travelling at very high speed.
Rita: A sports personality, Greg?

Greg: You'll have to wait and find out after the show, Rita, like everyone else! That's from seven to eight.

Rita: OK, OK. Well, on Thursday we have our regular concert tour report. Who is it this week, Greg?

Greg: It's one of your favourite bands, Sez U, and we'll be reporting on their tour of the Far East.

Rita: Which was quite a rave –

Greg: Yeah. The report, with some great music, is at nine-thirty Thursday.

Rita: I shan't miss it. Now, what about Student Scene this month?

Greg: Right, well we've got a special feature on what it's like to be a university student in the States. That'll be specially interesting to anyone thinking about doing some studying over there, I guess. That's on Friday the 17th at 4 p.m. Then on Monday the 20th at the same time, I shall be looking at how to get the best out of student travelcards, how to get around Europe for as little money as possible.

Rita: Sounds like useful stuff. And what about the retro theme? Are there any other features later on in the month which take us back?

Greg: Yeah, we're putting together a programme about people whose parents were big music names of the sixties and seventies, asking them what it was like to grow up with parents who'd many of them broken all the rules themselves.

Rita: Pretty hard to shock them, I guess.

Greg: Well, I think you're in for some surprises. Apparently, rock musicians can be surprisingly strict parents! Find out on Friday the 24th at five o'clock.

Rita: Right. What else?

Greg: On Monday the 27th at one o'clock, we've got an hour for reggae fans, when we feature the sound of Jamaica thirty years back. And the same evening, we've got a special competition, which is going to win someone an all expenses paid trip to Brazil. Can you imagine it?

Rita: Wow! What time?

Greg: The questions will be put out at nine, one, and seven. So everyone will have a chance to hear them.

Rita: Don't miss it, you guys. And I think our time's just about up, Greg, but I just want to mention a couple of fashion notes you've missed at the end of the month. First, on the 28th, I'll be visiting a shoe museum and talking to Anna Trent, the curator, to find out whether our modern shoe fashions are as new as we think they are. And on the 29th, I'll be visiting some of Manchester's top clubs to report on a revolution in style amongst dancers on the club scene. Want to come?

Greg: You bet you. And now we'd better get on with the music, hadn't we?

Rita: Yup. And . . .

[pause]

tone

Now you'll hear Part Two again.

[The recording is repeated.]

[pause]

That's the end of Part Two.
Now turn to Part Three.

PART 3   *You will hear five people talking about the jobs they'd like to have. For questions 19 to 23, choose from the list A to F what they describe. Use the letters only once. There is one extra letter which you do not need to use. You now have thirty seconds in which to look at Part Three.*

[pause]

tone

Woman: Yes, I've been, you know, thinking about getting back to work, now my children are at school all day. Um, I used to have a job, in the parks department at the council actually. It was very nice in some ways, you know, a nice atmosphere. I thought I might do um, some training, in planning people's um – like, what plants grow in different soils, and how to group them. I'd like going to meet them and discussing their – what they needed doing, you know, that sort of thing.

[pause]

Man: I want to do something that can make a difference to people. The trouble with this country is people don't really know what's going on. I mean, even things that affect, you know, their daily lives. So I could go out and really find out what's happening, meet the people who make the decisions and then produce articles that put the readers in the picture.

[pause]

Woman: I'm not afraid of hard work. I think some people go into, like, what do they call them, caring professions, thinking it's all about being kind and getting gratitude. Actually, I know it's actually quite, well, very, in fact sometimes, physically hard. And you have to study chemistry and biology and stuff. And sick people can be, well, you know, impatient, or depressed. But I still want to do it. I think if you can give, in your career, then you can't turn your back on it.

[pause]

Man: I'm very much what they call a 'people' person, so I'd like to feel I was one, um, part of a team, working to give the guests a good time, and I'd like to feel that I was perhaps their first contact as they came in, and I'm quite, you know, lively and smiley, I think. So that should help them to feel better, if they were worn out, you know, at the end of a long journey or something. And I think the leisure industry is growing, so that'd be good, career wise, I think.

[pause]

Man: I'm looking for something that will let me have contact with people. I've had several jobs in the past, mostly in offices, companies, sometimes quite interesting, but you're not dealing with the public. I'd like to be looking after people, not bits of paper. I think the sort of big store where people go to make, er, major purchases, furniture, you know, where the decisions will affect their lives for years, so you can really help them if you're well-informed about the products. I think that'd be quite rewarding, actually.

[pause]

tone

Now you'll hear Part Three again.

[The recording is repeated.]

[pause]

That's the end of Part Three.
Now turn to Part Four.

PART 4   *You will hear a conversation between a father, a mother and their son. For*
questions 24 to 30, decide who expresses each idea and mark F for the father,
M for the mother and S for the son.
You now have forty-five seconds in which to look at Part Four.

[pause]

tone

Son: Do you know the people at the house on the corner are building a swimming-pool in
their garden?

Father: Yeah, the Rawlings. They got a lot of money when their grandfather sold his business.

Mother: Did they? I suppose you think they're wasting it.

Son: No, it'd be great. Just think of getting up in the morning and having a swim before
breakfast.

Father: Ugh. Not in this climate. They'd be better off getting their roof fixed.

Mother: Oh, really. Don't be so sensible! But honestly, I don't know why they're bothering. If I
could afford a swimming-pool, you wouldn't catch me sticking around here.

Son: What?

Father: But this is a very popular area. We were very lucky to get this house at a reasonable
price.

Mother: Oh, it's very convenient, I know. But if you can afford to have a swimming-pool, you
could live somewhere much nicer.

Father: Like where?

Son: By the sea, for example?

Mother: Or anywhere, well out of town. Somewhere with beautiful views. Up in the hills away
from the traffic.

Father: But we wouldn't be able to get to work.

Son: She means, if we had so much money it didn't matter.

Father: Oh, I see. Oh, well – we can all dream, I suppose. I don't think even the Rawlings could
afford to give up working. I wonder if we'll be asked round when they've finished it?

Mother: Not if they hear us saying they should've spent it on the roof. But it is a funny thing to
do, really.

Son: I expect they just want to make people envy them.

Father: Yeah, they're either really concerned about what their neighbours think or –

Mother: – they have absolutely no idea how much people talk in this sort of neighbourhood!

Son: Yeah.

Mother: Well, anyway, we'd better clear this table. Someone's got homework, I presume?

Son: Okay.

Father: Right, yeah.

[pause]

tone

Now you'll hear Part Four again.

[The recording is repeated.]

[pause]

That is the end of Part Four.
There'll now be a pause of five minutes for you to copy your answers onto
the separate answer sheet.
I'll remind you when there's one minute left, so that you're sure to finish in
time.

[pause]

You have one more minute left.

[pause]

That's the end of the test. Please stop now. Your supervisor will now collect
all the question papers and answer sheets.
Goodbye.

Test 2 Key

Paper 1 Reading

Part 1
1 E   2 G   3 A   4 D   5 H   6 F   7 B

Part 2
8 B   9 C   10 A   11 C   12 C   13 D   14 B

Part 3
15 B   16 F   17 A   18 G   19 D   20 H
21 C

Part 4
22 D   23 E   24 C   25 B   26 A   27 C
28 A   29 F   30 B   31 E   32 A   33 B
34 D   35 A

Paper 2 Writing

Part 1 – Plan

> letter to A & J
>
> I heard about their party and want to ask
>
> our party at least 20
>
> does boat company provide:
>   transport to river?
>   food & drink?
>   music for dancing?
>
> what did it cost?
>
> thanks for trouble

Paper 3 Use of English

Award one mark for each correct answer, except in Part 3, where two marks are available, divided up as shown, for each answer.

Correct spelling is essential throughout. Ignore omission or abuse of capital letters. No half marks.

Part 1

1 C   2 B   3 D   4 A   5 B   6 D   7 C   8 A
9 D   10 D   11 B   12 C   13 B   14 D   15 A

Part 2

16 away   17 so   18 a   19 without   20 whole
21 everyone/everybody   22 what   23 if/when   24 something
25 in   26 for/to   27 up   28 which   29 how   30 to

Part 3

31 would/'d have difficulty (1) (in) finishing (1)
32 still lives in Spain(,) (1) does (1)
33 the meeting (1) without saying (1)
34 don't/wouldn't mind (1) lending (1)
35 is/'s rare for (1) Angus to (1)
36 my fault (1) we didn't/did not (1)
37 you have (1) (any) plans for (1)
38 doesn't take (1) after (1)
39 isn't/is not as/so (1) good as (1)
40 I hadn't/had not (1) given Dennis (1)

Part 4

41 through   42 ✓   43 it   44 rather   45 anything   46 own
47 ✓   48 at   49 ✓   50 so   51 how   52 is   53 because
54 up   55 me

Part 5

56 beings   57 selection   58 applicants   59 advice
60 unsuccessful   61 Similarly   62 inadequate   63 confidence
64 ability   65 honesty

Paper 4 Listening

Part 1

1 A   2 C   3 B   4 C   5 B   6 C   7 A   8 B

Part 2

9 careers   10 overseas/in other countries/abroad
11 visit companies (and)/businesses   12 (are) homeless

13 (student) common room   14 hot meals
15 (a) book exchange (throughout the college)
16 (a student) advice centre   17 accommodation   18 speakers

Part 3
19 E   20 B   21 D   22 A   23 F

Part 4
24 B   25 C   26 A   27 B   28 C   29 A   30 A

Tapescript *First Certificate Practice Test Two. Paper Four. Listening. Hello. I'm going to give you the instructions for this test. I'll introduce each part of the test and give you time to look at the questions. At the start of each piece, you'll hear this sound:*

tone

You'll hear each piece twice.
Remember, while you're listening, write your answers on the question paper. You'll have time at the end of the test to copy your answers onto the separate answer sheet.

The tape will now be stopped. Please ask any questions now, because you must not speak during the test.

[pause]

PART 1 *Now, open your question paper and look at Part One.*
You'll hear people talking in eight different situations. For questions 1 to 8, choose the best answer, A, B or C.

Question 1 One
This woman is talking on the telephone. Who is she speaking to?
A *her landlord*
B *an architect*
C *a builder*

[pause]

tone

Woman: I, um, I've looked up my copy of the thing I signed when I came here, and it's quite clear. I'm responsible for keeping things clean and so on, but it is up to you to see that it gets painted and things when necessary . . . No, it's not that. I'm not just asking because I want to change the colour scheme. The window frames will start to rot if you don't do it soon . . . Well, that's up to you, but I think you ought to have another look . . .

[pause]

tone

[The recording is repeated.]

[pause]

Question 2   Two
On holiday, you hear another tourist describing a journey. How did he feel?
A shocked
B embarrassed
C scared

[pause]

tone

Man: Anyway, they said it was very pretty, and well worth it because of the view up there. So, off we went, up that little road you can see from behind the hotel. And it wasn't a particularly good road anyway, and then we started twisting and turning about – ooh – and we were looking down into people's gardens and it felt – well, I just felt like we were going to go straight across their roofs half the time. I suppose you could get used to it if you grew up here, but not me. And coming down was even worse.

[pause]

tone

[The recording is repeated.]

[pause]

Question 3   Three
You hear these people talking in a café. Why did the man change his newspaper?
A the cost
B the opinions
C the quality of the writing

[pause]

tone

Woman: That's not the paper you used to get, is it?
Man: No.
Woman: I wondered who they'd attract by price-cutting.
Man: Ha ha. All ten pence of it. But I was getting tired of their attitude. It's very narrow.
Woman: Oh. How?
Man: Well, at least they look at more than one side of things in this, even if it isn't as well-written, on the whole.

[pause]

tone

[The recording is repeated.]

[pause]

Question 4   *Four*
              This woman is phoning a friend about the date of a meeting. Why has she
              called?
              A to apologise for changing it
              B to inform her about changing it
              C to explain the reason for changing it

              [pause]

              tone

Woman: It's about having to change the date of the committee meeting. I know you weren't best
              pleased about it, but the thing is, we've checked round and it really is the only date
              everyone can make. So that's got to be it really. I thought if you knew why, perhaps you
              wouldn't mind so much.

              [pause]

              tone

              [The recording is repeated.]

              [pause]

Question 5   *Five*
              You hear a girl talking about clothes. What is she describing?
              A a coat
              B a dress
              C a trouser suit

              [pause]

              tone

Girl: It was really a classic. It was in, um, this really soft, fine material, you know what I
              mean? And this incredible dark blue. There's a little, thin belt and it goes in tight at the
              waist and then it falls in these really deep folds – almost to the ankles. And then at the
              top – ooh – it's sleeveless and very plain, cut quite loose, but really beautifully finished.

              [pause]

              tone

              [The recording is repeated.]

              [pause]

Question 6   *Six*
              Listen to this film critic. What does he like least about the film?
              A the characters
              B the action scenes
              C the main story

              [pause]

              tone

Critic: I enjoyed it actually. It's not trying to be too clever. It's a straightforward adventure film with a, well, to be honest, pretty dull story, but it's well-acted. There's some sharp talking which is actually quite funny, a quite original car chase and a touching little love story woven through it. A pleasant way to relax for an hour or two if you get the opportunity, but not one to make a special trip for.

[pause]

tone

[The recording is repeated.]

[pause]

Question 7   *Seven*
You hear these people talking while queuing in a shop. What does the woman complain about?
A   *the payment system*
B   *the service*
C   *the quality of the goods*

[pause]

tone

Man: It's nearly ten minutes.
Woman: Oh, but it's much better than it was.
Man: Honestly, I thought things would have improved more than this. I mean there's not much of a range, is there?
Woman: What gets me, is why you still have to wait in line to choose things and then you have to wait in line again to pay. But you know, the people are much more relaxed and they try to help if they can.
Man: Mm.

[pause]

tone

[The recording is repeated.]

[pause]

Question 8   *Eight*
You hear these people talking about a book. Who is the book about?
A   *a poet*
B   *a songwriter*
C   *a journalist*

[pause]

tone

Male teenager: . . . but it doesn't really tell you what he was trying to say.

163

Female teenager:	Yes, it does. It's got all those letters and stuff. You can see that's where the ideas for the words came from.
Male:	Yeah, okay. But what about the tunes? He practically doesn't mention them.
Female:	And that piece in the paper said they're the most original part of his work.
Male:	I don't know. I suppose the writer didn't know so he just left out talking about them.

[pause]

tone

[The recording is repeated.]

[pause]

That's the end of Part One.
Now turn to Part Two.

PART 2 *You will hear two students who want to be chosen as student representative in their college. For questions 9 to 18, complete the notes. You will need to write a word or a short phrase.*
You now have forty-five seconds in which to look at Part Two.

[pause]

tone

Linda: Right, well, my name's Linda Goodyear and I'd like briefly to tell you why I think you should choose me as your rep. Um, these are the things I would try to do something about, try to improve, or, I mean, do.

So, er, I think we all know, the careers advice service needs, er, a bit of improvement. So I'd work to improve that. Especially, we need more practical advice about getting work experience, not in this country I mean, overseas. And another thing I think we should press for, is to have close links with businesses and companies where we can actually go on visits. I think we should try to get around, I mean not even just locally, but all over the Midlands, so we actually see a greater variety of ways of doing things rather than just hearing about them.

Then, um, the next thing I think is important is something I'm quite, er, involved with, myself. That's voluntary work with the homeless. I'd like to get more people here in the college involved, either directly, or I hope, with raising money.

And, er, last of all, er, I'd like to push the college authorities really hard for some new furniture for the student common room.

Thank you very much. Please vote for me.

Darren: Hi, everybody. Uh, I expect you may know, my name's Darren Whiting. Um, I'd really like to be your student rep this year, and well, here's what I'd try and do for you, for us. Um, first, I'd take on the canteen and try to stop them putting up the price of hot meals, as they've said they will.

Then, the next thing is, um, well, I'd like to organise a book exchange throughout the whole college, um, like already exists, um, in the maths department, to save money on expensive textbooks that we all have to have, but don't need for the whole course. Another thing we badly need in this college is a student advice centre. We need a place run by students for students, where people can drop in and get advice about any sort of problems, academic or welfare or whatever.

We also need to take on the college authorities on the subject of accommodation for students who need it. I mean, the situation at the moment is crazy, with no proper system for deciding who gets accommodation, or why. I want to change that.

And lastly, I want to get in more speakers, from all political backgrounds, and er, from industry and so on, to help get people more aware of, you know, what's going on in the world today. Because we'll all be out there soon, like it or not.

Please vote for me. Thanks for listening.

[pause]

tone

Now you'll hear Part Two again.

[The recording is repeated.]

[pause]

That's the end of Part Two.
Now turn to Part Three.

PART 3   *You will hear five people talking about sport.*
For questions 19 to 23, choose from the list A to F what they say. Use the letters only once. There is one extra letter which you do not need to use. You now have thirty seconds in which to look at Part Three.

[pause]

tone

Man: As you can imagine, this job involves spending most of my time alone, sitting at the word processor. So, I try and get up to the tennis club once or twice a week. I just want to move about a bit, make sure my legs and arms are still working. Doesn't really matter who I play with, most people are about the same standard. I really feel the difference if I miss a week though.

[pause]

Man: I don't really claim to be much of an expert. But at the end of the working week, I watch a good match on the box, or even go along to the local ground sometimes, and it just helps you forget all the stresses and strains, takes you out of yourself, you know what I mean?

[pause]

Woman: I don't think it was actually part of my original job description as such. When I started, someone said could I coach the under elevens sometimes, and I said yes, and somehow I've just gone on doing it, taking them to their matches and stuff. It's quite a pleasant change really, keeps me on the go, you know, once or twice a week.

[pause]

Boy: I, er my family moved here quite recently and, er, I didn't really bother much with sport before, but, um, I thought perhaps if I went along to this sports centre, you know, I could get to know a few different people from just the ones I see at school. Well, I quite enjoy it really, and I'm beginning to have a bit of a social life there as well, and I feel fitter too, which is an added bonus.

[pause]

Girl: It's a real laugh. We usually go every Saturday, and we wait outside and try to get a discount if we can. And we sometimes go round afterwards and try and get autographs. Well, that depends who's been playing of course. We all get worked up and have a good shout and get sore throats. It wouldn't be any good on your own, would it?

[pause]

tone

Now you'll hear Part Three again.

[The recording is repeated.]

[pause]

That's the end of Part Three.
Now turn to Part Four.

PART 4   *You will hear a local radio report about places to eat. For questions 24 to 30 choose the best answer A, B or C.*
You will have one minute in which to look at Part Four.

[pause]

tone

Presenter: And now that review of, er, local restaurants and suchlike where you might like to take the family over the bank holiday period. Caroline Chandler has been out and about sampling the goodies.

Caroline: Yes, I'm going to be dieting for weeks!

Presenter: So what have you found for us?

Caroline: Well, I've been to all sorts of places, so I hope there'll be something of interest for everyone. Starting at the bargain end, I went to Ali's sandwiches in Long Road. Ali does a great trade at lunchtimes, normally he's got office workers queuing out of the front door. He says he'll be open over the holiday weekend, and he's offering take-away picnic packs as well. You need to phone in your order for these the previous day, then you can collect first thing in the morning if you're having a day out. The number's double seven, double five, three two.

Presenter: And I'll be giving that phone number again at the end of the programme. So who's next, Caroline?

Caroline: Okay. Well, next I tried Chick'n'things, on the Market Square. This was down on my list as a fast food shop, and I must admit I thought it might be cheap and greasy. But at least, I thought, this'll be a good place for a quick something hot to eat on the way home from the cinema. What I found was, it's not particularly cheap, but the food's really quite tasty, so it's not in fact bad value. The main thing you have to remember though, is it's not actually all that fast, because they cook each order separately, so you have to hang about a bit . . .

Presenter: Right. So, what about if I want to sit down and eat?

Caroline: Well, I decided to go through a day, trying to find a different place for each meal!

Presenter:	So, where did you have breakfast?
Caroline:	Well, I'd always heard that the best breakfasts are the ones they give those long distance lorry drivers at transport cafés. So, I got up at six o'clock and drove out to Pat's Café on the bypass just north of town. I got a very friendly welcome and a free mug of tea, and then had the biggest meal I've ever eaten. It was brilliant!
Presenter:	Well done!
Caroline:	The only thing was, I had to postpone the rest of my research till the next day because I simply hadn't got room for any more.
Presenter:	I guess that's one of the dangers of being a food journalist.
Caroline:	I guess it is. Anyway, the next day I decided to start cautiously. I went for morning coffee to the Old Mill in Riverside Park. I have to say it wasn't the best I've ever had. It was instant, okay, well, that's a matter of opinion, but still. Anyway it was very pleasant sitting looking at the river, and I thought, I'd better have something to eat, just a light cake, you know. Again, I'm afraid it was just very sweet and artificial-tasting. I suppose they don't have to try so hard because people go to the park anyway, but I think it's a real pity.
Presenter:	I know what you mean. Specially as it's so popular with tourists. It gives them just the wrong impression, doesn't it?
Caroline:	Yes, anyway, after that I wanted something a bit healthier, and luckily I was heading for the Food Box. Do you know it?
Presenter:	It's on the corner of Orchard Street, isn't it? I must admit I thought the food might be a bit dull, all salads and vegetarian pies, and I'd feel about twenty years older than all the other customers.
Caroline:	Well, I think you're missing a treat. They've got a great range of stuff. Okay, no meat, but really you won't miss it, there are so many tasty hot and cold dishes. And people of all ages go there. I have to admit I'm a regular, so I know what I'm talking about.
Presenter:	Okay, perhaps I'll try it next time I'm passing, you never know. And so where did you have dinner?
Caroline:	Ah, well, for dinner I went to the new Italian restaurant on Castle Street, the Four Seasons.
Presenter:	And?
Caroline:	It was brilliant! We were a bit late, because we were ages trying to find somewhere to leave the car –
Presenter:	Yes, I know, I've had the same trouble in that part of town.
Caroline:	But they didn't mind a bit, nothing was too much trouble, and the food – I could talk about nothing else the whole of the next day. Yummy!
Presenter:	Well, Caroline, we're coming up to news time so I'll have to say thank you, and quickly give the number for Ali's picnic packs as I promised . . .

[pause]

tone

Now you'll hear Part Four again.

[The recording is repeated.]

[pause]

That is the end of Part Four.

There'll now be a pause of five minutes for you to copy your answers onto the separate answer sheet. I'll remind you when there's one minute left, so that you're sure to finish in time.

[pause]

You have one more minute left.

[pause]

That's the end of the test. Please stop now. Your supervisor will now collect all the questions papers and answer sheets.
Goodbye.

Test 3 Key

Paper 1 Reading

Part 1
1 C   2 E   3 G   4 B   5 A   6 D

Part 2
7 C   8 A   9 B   10 D   11 C   12 D   13 A   14 B

Part 3
15 F   16 D   17 A   18 G   19 E   20 C

Part 4
21 B   22 E   23 A   24 G   25 E   **26 and 27** D/F
28 A   29 D   30 C   31 A   32 B   **33 and 34** D/E   35 G
(Where there are two possible answers, these are interchangeable.)

Paper 2 Writing

Part 1 – Plan

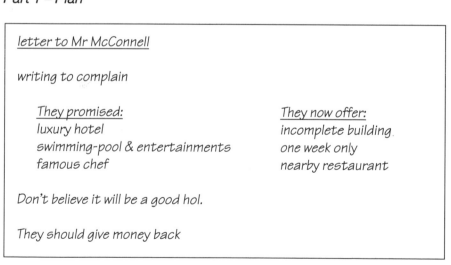

<u>letter to Mr McConnell</u>

writing to complain

    <u>They promised:</u>   <u>They now offer:</u>
    luxury hotel   incomplete building
    swimming-pool & entertainments   one week only
    famous chef   nearby restaurant

Don't believe it will be a good hol.

They should give money back

Paper 3 Use of English

Award one mark for each correct answer, except in Part 3, where two marks are available, divided up as shown, for each answer.

Correct spelling is essential throughout. Ignore omission or abuse of capital letters. No half marks.

Part 1

1 B   2 C   3 D   4 D   5 C   6 B   7 A   8 C   9 B
10 B   11 C   12 A   13 C   14 A   15 B

Part 2

16 as/when   17 at/to/toward(s)   18 in   19 one
20 nothing/little   21 as   22 has   23 well   24 on   25 ago
26 up   27 no   28 were/was   29 make/form   30 every

Part 3

31 don't feel like (1) spending (1)
32 best match (1) I have/'ve (ever) (1)
33 look up (1) to (1)
34 there was (1) anything she wanted (1)
35 in case Sally (1) doesn't/does not (1)
36 we had (1) remembered to take (1)
37 there was nothing OR nothing was (1) wrong (1)
38 in spite of (1) the/a change (1)
39 'd/had (1) better think (1)
40 time Jackie (1) went swimming (1)

Part 4

41 the   42 if   43 so   44 ✓   45 it   46 through
47 was   48 in   49 ✓   50 for   51 ✓   52 being   53 has
54 ever   55 ✓

Part 5

56 development   57 activities   58 frequently   59 behaviour
60 encourage   61 imagination   62 unexpected   63 explanation
64 relating/related   65 knowledge

Paper 4 Listening

Part 1

1 A   2 B   3 B   4 C   5 A   6 C   7 A   8 A

Part 2

9 Studio Design Centre   10 (his) mother's family   11 engines
12 liners/ships   13 physics   14 post office (queue)   15 clay
16 temperatures   17 (wall and floor) tiles   18 outdoors

Part 3

19 D   20 E   21 C   22 F   23 B

Part 4

24 Y   25 N   26 Y   27 N   28 Y   29 Y   30 N

Tapescript   *First Certificate Practice Test Three. Paper Four. Listening. Hello. I'm going to give you the instructions for this test. I'll introduce each part of the test and give you time to look at the questions. At the start of each piece, you'll hear this sound:*

tone

You'll hear each piece twice.
Remember, while you're listening, write your answers on the question paper. You'll have time at the end of the test to copy your answers onto the separate answer sheet.
The tape will now be stopped. Please ask any questions now, because you must not speak during the test.

[pause]

PART 1   *Now open your question paper and look at Part One.*
You'll hear people talking in eight different situations. For questions 1 to 8, choose the best answer, A, B or C.

Question 1   One
Listen to these colleagues talking. Why is the man going to Amsterdam?
A *on a business trip*
B *for a short holiday*
C *to study art*

[pause]

tone

Woman: Amsterdam, huh? Some people have all the luck. I've always wanted to do the museums there.

Man: Yeah, but you've got to remember I'm supposed to produce a guidebook at the end of it. My timetable won't let me enjoy the paintings – I'll be too busy checking which bus route they're on, and studying the price of souvenirs.

[pause]

tone

[The recording is repeated.]

[pause]

Question 2   *Two*
You're in a shop when you hear one of the assistants talking. What is he trying to do?
A persuade someone
B explain something
C correct a wrong idea

[pause]

tone

Shop assistant: Now, if I could just show you – a lot of people find it confusing. You see, these are what we call showerproof. They're what most people want. They'll keep out most of the wet, but they are what we call fashion garments, so – but nice, aren't they? But we do also have actual waterproofs too. But, um, they are more expensive. Well, if they're famous labels, anyway. So it depends really on how often you might get caught in a real rain storm, if you see what I mean?

[pause]

tone

[The recording is repeated.]

[pause]

Question 3   *Three*
You hear this reporter on the radio. Who is she going to meet?
A a fisherman
B a scientist
C a farmer

[pause]

tone

Reporter: Well, in recent years we've heard a lot about the damage to rivers and their fish stocks caused by pollution from agriculture. We've also been told that new laws have more or less put a stop to this kind of damage. Well, local fishermen say the farming community is ignoring them. So, I've asked pollution expert Dan Knox to meet me here on the river bank to carry out tests to see whether we can support the claims of either farmers or fishermen.

[pause]

tone

[The recording is repeated.]

[pause]

Question 4 Four
Listen to this teacher talking to a student. What is he giving?
A some advice
B an opinion
C some information

[pause]

tone

Teacher:	Now, I'm no great expert on exactly what's around nowadays –
Student:	Oh.
Teacher:	But I do know that there's an enormous variety. There are full-time schools, and ones that only operate in the summer. There are intensive courses and others which are just a holiday with a few lessons thrown in.
Student:	I see.
Teacher:	There is a file of leaflets in the library.
Student:	Oh, is there? I will look at them. Eh, thank you.
Teacher:	You're welcome.

[pause]

Question 5 Five
You hear this critic talking about an exhibition. What is its subject?
A life in a city
B the work of an architect
C rich and poor countries

[pause]

tone

Critic:	. . . and what I find most interesting, about what Pamela Eston has done, is to link together such a variety of images of the city, from, um, different stages, as it were, in its development. So that you get a feeling, um, of what living there's been like over the past five decades, and how that experience has changed. You know, she's got architect's plans and sketches from the fifties, alongside photos of present day homeless people, sheltering in the doorways of those same buildings.

[pause]

tone

[The recording is repeated.]

[pause]

Question 6 Six
You are listening to the news on the radio. Why was Brian Bolter on trial?
A for illegal gambling
B for accepting bribes
C for bribing players

[pause]

tone

Newsreader: . . . And news just in. Brian Bolter, the football manager accused of making illegal payments to players in order to fix the results of matches on which he had placed bets has been cleared of all charges. We're going straight over now to our correspondent outside the courtroom.

[pause]

tone

[The recording is repeated.]

[pause]

Question 7 *Seven*
You are on a bus when you hear this passenger get on. What does the driver offer to do?
A tell her when the bus reaches her stop
B point out the library
C stop outside the library

[pause]

tone

Passenger: Allard Road, please.
Driver: Which end?
Passenger: Um, I don't know. I want to go to the library.

Driver: That's the top you want then. Fifty p . . . Ta. The stop's just up the hill from it. I'll let you know which one.
Passenger: Oh, thank you.

[pause]

tone

[The recording is repeated.]

[pause]

Question 8 *Eight*
Listen to this boy talking about the town he lives in. What does he feel about it?
A He likes it.
B It's boring.
C It's old-fashioned.

[pause]

tone

Teenager: Yeah, I don't think my Dad and Mum like it here any more. When I was little, it was just a sleepy old market town. We all liked it then. But now there's, um, a lot of commercial development, specially electronics and such, so it's changed a lot. They don't feel at home here like they did. But me, I've changed too. I've just about got a job lined up for when I leave school. I do think my parents would like to move really, but they know what I'd feel about that, so they'll probably stay – until I leave school, anyway.

[pause]

tone

[The recording is repeated.]

[pause]

That's the end of Part One.
Now turn to Part Two.

PART 2 *You will hear a radio journalist interviewing Frank Irvine, a successful potter. For questions 9 to 18, complete the notes. You will need to write a word or a short phrase.*
You now have forty-five seconds in which to look at Part Two.

[pause]

tone

Journalist: Now, I'm with Frank Irvine whose current exhibition here at the Studio Design Centre in North London is attracting quite a bit of attention. And about time too, I should think. Um, Frank, I hope you won't mind my saying, but you're not all that young to be having a first major show in London?

Frank: No, it's quite true. I was born in 1948, after all.

Journalist: In Glasgow, was that?

Frank: Actually no. My father was Austrian and I was born there.

Journalist: Really?

Frank: But my father died while I was still a baby and my mother, who was a Scot, returned with me to be near her own family.

Journalist: Ah. And when did you start getting interested in making pots?

Frank: Well, as a child I was into engines in a big way. Anything noisy and smelly, my mother would say. And out of that I developed an ambition to work in the shipyards.

Journalist: Oh, did you?

Frank: I wanted to be solving design problems with some of those great liners they used to build. A bit late in the day perhaps. I even started a degree in physics, um, at Edinburgh. But I think by the time I was about twenty I was already aware that there might be something else I wanted to do. I didn't know what, that's all.

Journalist: So, what did you do?

Frank: Well, I started travelling. Er, initially, to find out more about my father's background, and then I went to the Middle East and on to India. Where I met my wife, Carole.

Journalist: And her father, I believe?

Frank: Yes. We were all waiting in the post office in um, Bombay, actually, and we just struck up a conversation. And soon after that we came back to England and I was visiting them quite a lot and seeing her father working –

Journalist: He being the potter Arthur Saunders –

Frank:	Right. Sorry. And eventually I plucked up courage to ask if I could have a go. And well, once I'd started, of course, I couldn't stop. I soon got very interested in experimenting with different kinds of clay.
Journalist:	From all over the world.
Frank:	Yes, that's right. And then I started playing around with patterns and colours and using very, very high temperatures to produce some pretty unique effects.
Journalist:	And this was quite some time ago?
Frank:	Oh, I've been playing about with this since the 1970s. I started with quite small bowls, you know, small domestic objects, then I wanted to try making designs on a larger scale, but still something that might find its way into a home, rather than a museum, so I tried wall tiles. You know, the sort of thing you can stick up in the kitchen or bathroom. Then I got onto the idea of them being used outdoors, like on patios and so on, so they got bigger and bigger. And other people like them too.
Journalist:	They certainly do. And I can see why.

[pause]

tone

Now you'll hear Part Two again.

[The recording is repeated.]

[pause]

That's the end of Part Two.
Now turn to Part Three.

PART 3   *You will hear five people being interviewed about how they spend their free time.*
For questions 19 to 23, choose from the list of activities A to F. Use the letters only once. There is one extra letter which you do not need to use. You now have thirty seconds in which to look at Part Three.

[pause]

tone

Interviewer:	And in your free time?
Woman:	When I have any! Well, I suppose it'll be better after I take the exam. But, well, I try to go to a club where there is a quite big pool I can use –
Interviewer:	Uh-huh.
Woman:	– and, eh, I try to do perhaps fifty lengths twice a week, I think it's one of the best ways –
Interviewer:	Sure.
Woman:	But that's all, at the moment, really.

[pause]

Interviewer:	And how do you relax?
Man:	I like to drive up into the hills with a sketch-book in my pocket.
Interviewer:	Yeah?
Man:	I like the idea of walking, but I soon get bored, or tired, so –

| Interviewer: | Yes. |
| Man: | – I soon find a sheltered corner with a nice view and try to get it on paper. |

[pause]

Interviewer:	So what do you do?
Boy:	I belong to this Youth Club, see?
Interviewer:	Yeah?
Boy:	And we put plays on and, you know, things –
Interviewer:	You take part in them?
Boy:	Well, just little parts so far. But we might do, like, a rock musical next year and I'm after something, the main bad guy, in that. You don't have to do any singing in it, luckily. It'd be really good.

[pause]

Interviewer:	And how do you relax?
Woman:	When I can –
Interviewer:	Of course.
Woman:	– now I don't have to regard feeding people as a duty –
Interviewer:	Not day in, day out.
Woman:	Right. I love to have a few friends round at the weekend, then spend lots of time dreaming up a menu, try out new dishes, see what they think. It's a nice change.

[pause]

| Interviewer: | And what's your ideal way to spend free time? |
| Man: | Uh, I get out a pair of good old boots I had since college, and uh, just head on out into the country. |

Interviewer:	Yeah?
Man:	I like to spend a while wandering around.
Interviewer:	Alone?
Man:	Yeah. But I like to take a break and talk to the locals sometimes. It's the only way to meet genuine country people, get out there and find them. And I get some good exercise, clear my head.

[pause]

tone

Now you'll hear Part Three again.

[The recording is repeated.]

[pause]

That's the end of Part Three.
Now turn to Part Four.

PART 4 *You will hear part of a radio documentary about running a small business. For questions 24 to 30, decide whether the idea was stated or not and mark Y for Yes, or N for No.*
You now have forty-five seconds in which to look at Part Four.

[pause]

tone

Presenter: Lastly today on *Talking Shop* we're looking into getting started. You'd like to be your own boss? Well, you certainly need to look before you leap. John Apsley is the manager of a high street bank in the north of England.

John: There are quite a lot of people who just aren't suited to running their own business. I get a lot of people come to me wanting a start-up loan. They haven't got a clue. They haven't studied their market. They haven't got a business plan. It's not enough if their friends like their home-made cakes, or their computer game or whatever. I tell them to go away and do their homework. It sounds hard, but I'm doing them a good turn. If they're any good, they'll be back. If not, well, we're both better off.

Presenter: So what do you do? Sally has a T-shirt shop in Wilton.

Sally: I went to see my Dad's accountant. She was a big help, didn't, like, just make me feel stupid, like he does sometimes. And she told me how to set things out, like a business plan, you know, to impress the bank manager. And he was, I think. Dad says he can be really fierce, but he was very helpful to me and I got lots of advice and a loan.

Presenter: Otherwise . . . ? Megan Bracewell.

Megan: It took me years to realise I wasn't really earning a living, because my paperwork was such a mess. You know, I was just bashing on, turning out the goods, and I'd never done any real costing. I didn't know how. Then I got this enormous tax bill. It nearly finished us off completely, about three years ago. Anyway, we just about managed to pay it, but it gave us such a fright, we had a big shake up and I think we've survived. But only just!

Presenter: And if you do have problems? John Apsley again.

John: Another thing is they don't get in touch before there's a crisis. They just sit there, watching it develop, and then come rushing round when, likely as not, there's nothing more to be done. Then of course it's the bank's fault. But we can't help if the guy's not keeping us properly up to date, can we?

Presenter: As Colin Sharpe discovered.

Colin: I had this big export order. I phoned the bank, and I said, look, I've got this big order. It's the biggest I've ever had. I need to buy in a lot more raw materials, quickly like. Can I have some more credit? And they said, er, er, look at the file, basically no, you're extended as far as you can. It's too much of a risk. Course what I didn't tell them was who this customer was. Didn't occur to me that that might make a difference, did it? Then I just happened to see the assistant manager that evening, I was having a bit of a moan at him, and he says, who did you say? Course we'll be able to help you – just in time – ridiculous!

Presenter: Of course it helps to have a good relationship with the bank. But what else really matters? When you're working from dawn to dusk just to get the product out to the customers, it's difficult to find the time to attend to the other little details – John Apsley.

John: My clients in the computer world may not thank me for saying this, but you don't need all kinds of fancy systems to run a small business. What you need is to follow a simple routine and keep records. I'd rather see a single notebook and a shoe box full of receipts which are used every day than some expensive accounting software that nobody's had time to keep up to date.

Presenter: Well, that's telling you, as they say. Next week, we'll be looking at the subject of employment . . .

[pause]

tone

Now you'll hear Part Four again.

[The recording is repeated.]

[pause]

That is the end of Part Four.

There'll now be a pause of five minutes for you to copy your answers onto the separate answer sheet.
I'll remind you when there's one minute left, so that you're sure to finish in time.

[pausc]

You have one more minute left.

[pause]

That's the end of the test. Please stop now. Your supervisor will now collect all the question papers and answer sheets.
Goodbye.

Test 4 Key

Paper 1 Reading

Part 1
1 C   2 E   3 A   4 H   5 G   6 B   7 D

Part 2
8 B   9 D   10 B   11 D   12 C   13 A   14 A

Part 3
15 C   16 H   17 A   18 D   19 G   20 E   21 B

Part 4
22 B   23 G   24 D   25 G   26 F   27 A   28 D
29 C   30 A   31 G   32 E   33 G   34 D   35 B

Paper 2 Writing

Part 1 – Plan

> letter to Katarina
>
> why I'm writing – impossible for friend to come
>
> because –
> • cheap accommodation booked last year, expensive now
> • theatre and sightseeing trips all fully booked
>
> but most important – a beginner – wouldn't enjoy anything – needs good English for lectures, theatre
> (old-fashioned language difficult)
>
> v. sorry – next year perhaps

Paper 3 Use of English

Award one mark for each correct answer, except in Part 3, where two marks are available, divided up as shown, for each answer.

Correct spelling is essential throughout. Ignore omission or abuse of capital letters. No half marks.

Part 1

1 D   2 B   3 A   4 C   5 A   6 A   7 D   8 B   9 A
10 C   11 B   12 B   13 D   14 C   15 A   —

Part 2

16 side   17 may/might/could/would   18 As   19 known
20 the/his/this   21 made   22 if   23 of   24 its   25 there
26 brought   27 where   28 who/that   29 Until/Till/Before
30 to/onto/into

Part 3

31 said a/one word (1) to me (1) OR told me (1) a single)/one word (1)
32 didn't appear (1) to be (1)
33 had to (1) turn it down (1)
34 advised Carl (1) not to trust (1)
35 have no/haven't any idea (1) why (1)
36 the cheapest desk (1) you have (1)
37 was being (1) examined by (1)
38 make him (1) wash (1)
39 miss getting/receiving (1) letters (1); [miss hearing = 1 mark]
40 is expected (1) to accept (1)

Part 4

41 ✓   42 past   43 at   44 those   45 up   46 must
47 just   48 ✓   49 same   50 they   51 ✓   52 an
53 own   54 very   55 from

Part 5

56 decision   57 professional   58 photography   59 reasonably
60 allowance   61 agency   62 useful   63 sales   64 original
65 publisher('s)

Paper 4 Listening

Part 1

1 A   2 B   3 C   4 B   5 A   6 C   7 C   8 A

Part 2

9 (a) couple (of)/two/2   10 bee-keeping   11 (the) harbour

12 transport   13 iron   14 photographs   15 soft play area
16 adventure playground   17 science   18 Fire and Flames

Part 3

19 F   20 B   21 C   22 A   23 D

Part 4

24 F   25 T   26 T   27 F   28 T   29 F   30 T

Tapescript   *First Certificate Practice Test Four. Paper Four. Listening. Hello. I'm going to give you the instructions for this test. I'll introduce each part of the test and give you time to look at the questions. At the start of each piece, you'll hear this sound:*

tone

You'll hear each piece twice.
Remember, while you're listening, write your answers on the question paper. You'll have time at the end of the test to copy your answers onto the separate answer sheet.
The tape will now be stopped. Please ask any questions now, because you must not speak during the test.

[pause]

Now open your question paper and look at Part One.

PART 1   *You'll hear people talking in eight different situations. For questions 1 to 8, choose the best answer, A, B or C.*

Question 1   *One*
You hear this man talking on the radio about a politician. When did he get to know her?
A at school
B at university
C in his first job

[pause]

tone

Man: When I was at university, um, I'd hear of her from her cousins and things. She was, oh, travelling round the world at that time – making a name for herself already. She sounded very grand and successful to me. Yup, I found it hard to connect such a person with the girl – I used to help her with her homework, you know. Huh. And then she invited me to join the team she was putting together for her first election. I was very excited that she even remembered me. But I don't see so much of her now.

[pause]

tone

[The recording is repeated.]

[pause]

Question 2   *Two*
You're in a restaurant when you overhear this conversation. What is wrong with the food?
A *It's stale.*
B *It's overcooked.*
C *It's the wrong order.*

[pause]

tone

Mother:	I'm afraid I must ask you to change my daughter's meal.
Waitress:	Madam?
Mother:	She can't eat this pizza. It's absolutely rock hard. It must've been sitting at the back of the oven all day.
Waitress:	I'm very sorry. I can't think how it can have happened. I'll get another straight away.
Mother:	Thank you so much.

[pause]

tone

[The recording is repeated.]

[pause]

Question 3   *Three*
You hear the weather forecast on the radio. How long will the bad weather last?
A *until midday tomorrow*
B *until tomorrow evening*
C *until the day after tomorrow*

[pause]

tone

Weatherman:	And, oh dear, here is a warning of severe weather conditions affecting the whole country. Starting tonight, violent storms will reach all northerly regions by the end of tomorrow morning and elsewhere in the country by the end of the day. They will continue for a further twenty-four hours at least, with high winds and very heavy rain. Storm damage is likely in hilly areas and drivers of high-sided vehicles should avoid exposed roads and bridges. So do take care, won't you?

[pause]

tone

[The recording is repeated.]

[pause]

Question 4   *Four*
You are in a bank when you hear this conversation. What does the woman want to do?
A *borrow some money*
B *take out some of her money*
C *transfer her money to a new account*

[pause]

tone

Customer:	Um, it's about my savings account . . .
Cashier:	Yes?
Customer:	What I was wondering is whether there's any reason why I can't withdraw some money from it before the end of the year. I mean, I know you're advised . . .
Cashier:	Well, you'd lose interest of course, and you have to give a week's notice, but as long as there's a minimum of hundred pounds left in, it's no problem.
Customer:	Oh, right, well in that case, can I give notice now for two hundred pounds?

[pause]

tone

[The recording is repeated.]

[pause]

Question 5   *Five*
Listen to this man describing a concert. What did he like about it?
A *the first part*
B *the songs*
C *the instrumental section*

[pause]

tone

Man:	Oh, it was dreadful. You know, they had this group in the middle, doing these songs from the sixties. They were rubbish then, even. I don't know why they brought them back. And all the rest was just really poor quality sort of jazz stuff, no singing, no atmosphere. They'd started with a couple of classic tunes from the thirties, and I'd thought oh, this is quite promising, someone's thought out the programme here, but they hadn't. It just got worse and worse.

[pause]

tone

[The recording is repeated.]

[pause]

Question 6   *Six*
Listen to these language teachers. What may cause a problem for students,
according to the woman?
A violence
B prejudice
C loneliness

[pause]

tone

Teacher 1:   But what better way to learn a language?
Teacher 2:   I know, but people's feelings can be important, too.
Teacher 1:   What? Racist attitudes? That's not really likely, is it?
Teacher 2:   You misunderstand me. I meant, er, they'll be a long way from home, often alone – they may find it pretty tough . . .
Teacher 1:   Well, any big city can be dangerous if you're not sensible but . . .
Teacher 2:   No, just emotionally, that's all I'm saying.

[pause]

tone

[The recording is repeated.]

[pause]

Question 7   *Seven*
Some friends are talking about a film. What does the boy emphasise about the
director?
A She's Indian.
B She's a woman.
C She's young.

[pause]

tone

Girl: I thought it was a bit obvious. You know, coming to terms with a different way of life, Indian communities and stuff, I mean I know there aren't so many women doing that kind of thing . . .
Boy: No, I know what you mean, but what's interesting is, I mean, you know she's not just a woman, she's not much older than us. Did you know that?
Girl: Really? Wow, imagine me going to India and saying 'I want to make a film' – just like that!

[pause]

tone

[The recording is repeated.]

[pause]

Eight
You hear this woman talking about a colleague on the phone. What has he done?
A *passed his driving test*
B *bought a car*
C *started driving lessons*

[pause]

tone

Woman: Yes . . . apparently, he'd failed several times . . . stopped talking about it,
mm . . . seemed a bit mean . . . so last time he just put his hand in his pocket and
'happened' to find the car keys in it, know what I mean? . . . Yeah, passed last week,
apparently . . . it was rather sweet, I thought . . . and his wife'll be relieved . . . no, she
used to have to keep giving him lifts . . .

[pause]

tone

[The recording is repeated.]

[pause]

That's the end of Part One.
Now turn to Part Two.

PART 2 *You will hear a radio feature about the city of Bristol. For questions 9 to 18,*
complete the notes. You will need to write a word or a short phrase. You now
have forty-five seconds in which to look at Part Two.

[pause]

tone

Teresa: Hello again. This is Teresa Shaw with *Where Next?*, our weekly travel and leisure spot.
This week I've been looking at the attractions of Bristol, in the west of England. This
ancient seaport has a lot to recommend it.
First of all, I'd like to tell you about Ashton Court. Now this is a lovely old house set in
350 hectares of parkland only a couple of miles from the city centre. All sorts of events
go on there, or you can just relax in the grounds. There's a Visitor Centre where you can
learn about the history of the house and park, and if you like honey, you'll enjoy the
exhibition about bee-keeping over the last one hundred years.
For a different kind of history, you can make your way to the Maritime Museum and
the Industrial Museum, both in the harbour area of Bristol. The latter houses, among
other things, a special collection of all sorts of means of transport, from horse-drawn
carriages to a helicopter. And just along the road is the S.S. Great Britain, the
revolutionary ocean-going iron ship built in Bristol in 1843. This is a unique opportunity
to find out about life at sea a hundred and fifty years ago. Definitely not to be missed.
But if all that sounds a bit mechanical for your tastes, there's always the zoo. As well
as many fascinating animals, the zoo offers a variety of special events from bird flying
displays to treasure hunts to an exhibition by some of the world's top wildlife

photographers. You can phone for a special events brochure from March onwards. For young children, there is a special soft play area, and for slightly older ones with extra energy to burn off, there's an adventure playground. There are plenty of places to picnic or you can eat at the Pelican Restaurant. Wheelchair users are made welcome too, I'm happy to say. And remember, by supporting the zoo, you're also supporting its vital conservation work.

Lastly, still with the theme of education made enjoyable, there's the Exploratory. This is the place for a really different day out. It's full of exhibits which offer the chance for hands-on experience of the world of science. Each exhibit is a simple experiment which you carry out for yourself. Learn about how sound works, how we see colours, play with electricity – safely, of course – and masses of other scientific topics. There are also special live shows and workshops, such as *Bubble Magic* and *Fire and Flames*. There's also a shop full of amazing books and toys. It's easy to reach . . .

[pause]

tone

Now you'll hear Part Two again.

[The recording is repeated.]

[pause]

That's the end of Part Two.
Now turn to Part Three.

PART 3 *You will hear five people talking about feelings they have experienced. For questions 19 to 23, choose from the list of feelings A to F. Use the letters only once. There is one extra letter which you do not need to use. You now have thirty seconds in which to look at Part Three.*

[pause]

tone

Man: Anyway, I jumped off the train and I was going as fast as I could along the platform, 'cause I had this interview and I thought I was going to miss the bus into town, you know. This old guy was getting out of the next carriage and I half bumped into him, and he said, 'Watch where you're going, young fellow' and I just shouted 'Oh push off' and ran on. And then I got to the interview, and there he was, behind the desk. God, it was awful. I just wanted the earth to open up and swallow me.

[pause]

Woman: We hadn't actually invited him, but we didn't mind too much at first. At first he was quite good, helping and things, but that soon wore off. And then he never seemed to have any money on him when we went out anywhere. And it's not as if he's short, he's got a good job. Then I found out he'd been making phone calls all round the world. I tell you, he's a complete waste of space. He won't get through our door again.

[pause]

Man: I was living in the States for a while, looking after this friend's house while he was away on a business trip. One night as I was just drifting off to sleep the doorbell went. I looked out of the window, couldn't see anyone, decided I'd dreamt it. Just getting back into bed when it rang again. Still no sign of anyone. It took ages to get off again and then it woke me again. By then I was in such a state I couldn't sleep at all. Just sat there with the light on all night. I never did find out what had caused it.

[pause]

Woman: When we were little, we used to spend the summer holidays with some cousins in France. It was a lovely opportunity for us, although we didn't really appreciate it as much as we should have at the time. Anyway, I once broke some old vase that was quite valuable, and everyone blamed the dogs. No one ever even suggested it might have been me, but I felt dreadful all that summer. They all thought I was ill, but it was just a bad conscience.

[pause]

Man: Yeah, the course was good. Some of the teachers are, you know, quite well-known people. The only thing was – well, I know I knew the other students but, um, I haven't actually been away on my own anywhere for so long. I kept reminding myself it was a great chance, I mean, I was lucky to be there – but all the time there was this clock inside of me, you know, telling me how much longer before I could be on my way back.

[pause]

tone

Now you'll hear Part Three again.

[The recording is repeated.]

[pause]

That's the end of Part Three.
Now turn to Part Four.

PART 4   *You will hear part of a radio interview with Sharon Walker, a young woman who has recently changed her career. For questions 24 to 30, decide whether the statements are true or false and mark **T** for True, or **F** for False. You now have forty-five seconds in which to look at Part Four.*

[pause]

tone

Interviewer: So, Sharon, the big question, why did you decide to give up tennis?

Sharon: Well, it wasn't just something that happened overnight, of course. But three years ago, I'd been playing in a lot of big competitions, and I was very tired, I wanted to get away and have a good rest.

Interviewer: This was after the French Open?

Sharon: That's right. And I realised that actually I couldn't in fact do that because I was already fixed to play in various places all round the world for months ahead and I just had to go on.

Interviewer: And you did. And went on winning, too.

Sharon: Yes. It was actually a very good year for me professionally. But I became increasingly

	aware that I was playing because I had to. I mean, when I was younger, I just loved it. Not just playing, I mean, but everything, the competition, the travel . . .
Interviewer:	And you made a lot of money, too, didn't you?
Sharon:	I was a millionaire at eighteen. But don't misunderstand me. I'd play matches again tomorrow if that was all there was to it. Just walk out onto the court and start playing. I mean, I do still like to get a game in every day if I can. But I was worn out by all the other stuff. Um, I think when you're just a kid, at first it's funny when you go out to get a burger and next day it's all in the papers. But as you mature, well, as I did, you begin to need the space to develop, to find out about who you are, to explore relationships. And that's hard to do when there's always some journalist ready to tell everyone who you've been seeing and what you said and did, when you're still only nineteen. You lose the right to a private life. So, in the end, I thought, okay, maybe I've got another ten years at the top – if I'm lucky, then I'll still be wondering who I am and I'll have lost that ten years before I even begin to find out.
Interviewer:	So you got out?
Sharon:	Yeah.
Interviewer:	And you had to put up with some fairly unkind comments.
Sharon:	Uh-huh. There were some pretty mean things in the papers, and even some other players, I guess they thought I'd let them down in some way. After all, I was kind of admitting that tennis might not be the most important thing in the world, and that wasn't something that they were ready to accept, but I wasn't saying anything about what they were doing, I was only doing what seemed right for me.
Interviewer:	Do you have many regrets?
Sharon:	Well, it'd be less than the truth if I said none at all. Of course there are times when I wonder if I made a big mistake. But I have a good marriage, a lovely daughter and a job which I enjoy, so they never last more than a few moments.
Interviewer:	Ah, yes, your daughter –
Sharon:	Maisie.
Interviewer:	Do you hope Maisie will be a tennis star one day? Will you encourage her?
Sharon:	Um, that's a tricky one. I wouldn't discourage her, if she had talent. But it's getting more and more difficult to keep a balance. The level of competition is so high, and it starts so early now, I think it's very difficult for kids to hold on to a normal life if they're in serious training. So – let's say, I won't break my heart if she never gets further than the local club.
Interviewer:	Sharon, thank you for talking to us.
Sharon:	My pleasure.

[pause]

tone

Now you'll hear Part Four again.

[The recording is repeated.]

[pause]

That is the end of Part Four.
There'll now be a pause of five minutes for you to copy your answers onto the separate answer sheet.
I'll remind you when there's one minute left, so that you're sure to finish in time.

[pause]

You have one more minute left.

[pause]

That's the end of the test. Please stop now. Your supervisor will now collect all the question papers and answer sheets.

Goodbye.

CAMBRIDGE
EXAMINATIONS, CERTIFICATES AND DIPLOMAS
ENGLISH AS A FOREIGN LANGUAGE

University of Cambridge
Local Examinations Syndicate
International Examinations

Examination Details	9999/01		99/D99
Examination Title	First Certificate in English		
Centre/Candidate No.	AA999/9999		
Candidate Name	A.N. EXAMPLE		

• Sign here if the details above are correct

X

• Tell the Supervisor now if the details above
  are not correct

Candidate Answer Sheet: FCE Paper 1 Reading

Use a pencil

Mark ONE letter for each
question.

For example, if you think **B** is
the right answer to the
question, mark your answer
sheet like this:

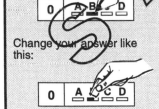

Change your answer like
this:

1	A B C D E F G H I
2	A B C D E F G H I
3	A B C D E F G H I
4	A B C D E F G H I
5	A B C D E F G H I

6	A B C D E F G H I
7	A B C D E F G H I
8	A B C D E F G H I
9	A B C D E F G H I
10	A B C D E F G H I
11	A B C D E F G H I
12	A B C D E F G H I
13	A B C D E F G H I
14	A B C D E F G H I
15	A B C D E F G H I
16	A B C D E F G H I
17	A B C D E F G H I
18	A B C D E F G H I
19	A B C D E F G H I
20	A B C D E F G H I

21	A B C D E F G H I
22	A B C D E F G H I
23	A B C D E F G H I
24	A B C D E F G H I
25	A B C D E F G H I
26	A B C D E F G H I
27	A B C D E F G H I
28	A B C D E F G H I
29	A B C D E F G H I
30	A B C D E F G H I
31	A B C D E F G H I
32	A B C D E F G H I
33	A B C D E F G H I
34	A B C D E F G H I
35	A B C D E F G H I

Paper 3

For Supervisor's use only

Shade here if the candidate is
ABSENT or has WITHDRAWN

➡ ▭ ↩

Examination Details	9999/03	99/D99

Examination Title First Certificate in English

Centre/Candidate No. AA999/9999

Candidate Name A.N. EXAMPLE

• Sign here if the details above are correct

X

• Tell the Supervisor now if the details above
  are not correct

Candidate Answer Sheet: FCE Paper 3 Use of English

Use a pencil

For **Part 1**: Mark ONE letter for each question.

For example, if you think **C** is the
right answer to the question,
mark your answer sheet like this:

0 [A] [B] [C] [D]

For **Parts 2, 3, 4** and **5**: Write your
answers in the spaces next to the
numbers like this:

0 | *example*

Part 1					Part 2		Do not write here
1	A	B	C	D	16		16
2	A	B	C	D	17		17
3	A	B	C	D	18		18
4	A	B	C	D	19		19
5	A	B	C	D	20		20
6	A	B	C	D	21		21
7	A	B	C	D	22		22
8	A	B	C	D	23		23
9	A	B	C	D	24		24
10	A	B	C	D	25		25
11	A	B	C	D	26		26
12	A	B	C	D	27		27
13	A	B	C	D	28		28
14	A	B	C	D	29		29
15	A	B	C	D	30		30

Turn
over
for
Parts
3 - 5
➡

Part 3		Do not write here		
31		31 0	1	2
32		32 0	1	2
33		33 0	1	2
34		34 0	1	2
35		35 0	1	2
36		36 0	1	2
37		37 0	1	2
38		38 0	1	2
39		39 0	1	2
40		40 0	1	2

Part 4		Do not write here
41		41
42		42
43		43
44		44
45		45
46		46
47		47
48		48
49		49
50		50
51		51
52		52
53		53
54		54
55		55

Part 5		Do not write here
56		56
57		57
58		58
59		59
60		60
61		61
62		62
63		63
64		64
65		65

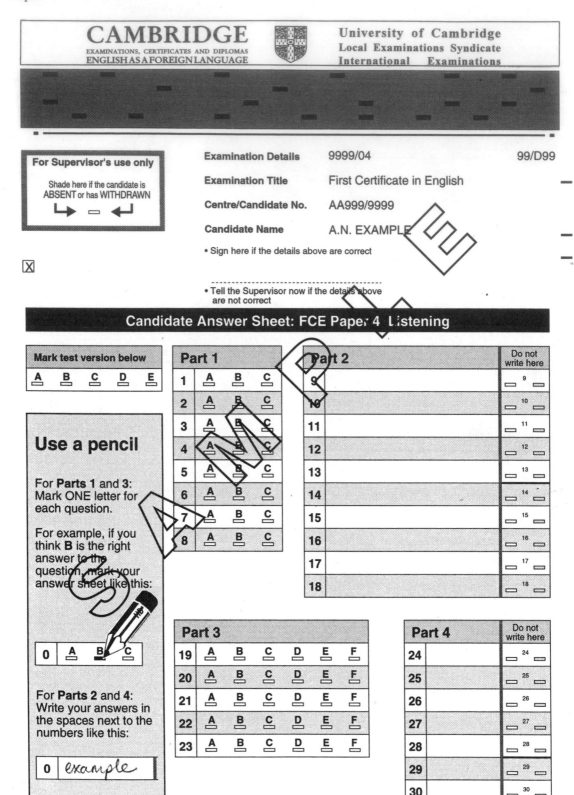

© UCLES/K&J   *You may photocopy this page.*